The Ethical
Psychic Vampire

Raven Kaldera

The Ethical Psychic Vampire

Raven Kaldera

Ellhorn Press
Hubbardston, Massachusetts

Asphodel Press
12 Simond Hill Road
Hubbardston, MA 01452

The Ethical Psychic Vampire
2nd Edition
© 2008 Raven Kaldera
ISBN 978-0-578-00790-8

Printed in cooperation with
Lulu Enterprises, Inc.
860 Aviation Parkway, Suite 300
Morrisville, NC 27560

*Dedicated to my daughter Jess
and all the other young vampires out there*

Acknowledgements

Many thanks to all the folks who put themselves and their words out there in order to fill out the experiences in this book. Thanks also for Bella for being patient with me, and Joshua for keeping me going.

Contents

Introduction to the Second Edition

Of all the books I've ever put out, this one is probably considered the weirdest. My books on shamanism, on Pagan religion, even on the various permutations of BDSM were all geared to a specific audience, people who understood and wanted the information, and were eager for it. Even if others, upon picking up those books, were bewildered or horrified, I knew that there was a core of people who would defend them. This book, on the other hand, was a complete act of faith. It was information that I'd won, hard-won even, over the years of coping with this aspect of myself. I knew that it needed to be out there. I didn't know if anyone else would agree, or if it would just fall into the void.

No "regular" press would take it, so I saved up money and put it out through print-on-demand. Back then I didn't know what I know now about self-publishing, so that was an act of faith as well. I didn't expect any response at all. I certainly didn't expect the people who wrote me and thanked me for putting all this into print.

Occasionally it was people who had heretofore identified as vampires, but more often it was their friends, lovers, partners, family, or counselors who were reading it and saying, "Yes! Now I know what's going on with Joe!" Or Mary, or Consuela, or Bart, or whoever. Usually they'd complained about the person in their life who exhibited telltale symptoms, and a friend said, "You have to read this book." What I wish I knew, in many of these cases, was whether the poor vampire in question got something out of it—some help, some aid in controlling a difficult and ambivalent gift.

Because this book was written, first and foremost, for the vampires themselves. It still is, even though its message may be rough against the nerves. I wrote it deliberately in plain, strong language, like I'd say to someone I was counseling, looking them directly in the eye. You need to do this, or this is going to happen. You think it won't, or you think it won't matter, but it will. Trust me on this. I didn't get these grey hairs for nothing.

As we go into the second printing of this book, little has changed. The message as it stands is still good, and I see no reason to alter it. What I have added is further words from real people, which means more perspective, making the work deeper and broader and bringing it further into vivid color. I still don't pull punches, but the voices of others have helped to explain those punches a little more compassionately.

To all the vampires: may you find joy in discipline, and mastery in mastering yourself. And for all who stay with us and love us ... thank you. You do the world a greater service than you know.

RAVEN KALDERA
NOVEMBER 2008
Hubbardston MA

1
Psychic Vampires

Everyone knows at least one psychic vampire. If you have a wide variety of friends, you probably know more than one. Psychic workers warn you against them. New Age counselors shake their heads and talk about unenlightened or unevolved beings. People who don't even believe in that stuff can nonetheless pick out the one person who makes them feel mysteriously drained, and they avoid them. When you pass them, you may feel your skin crawl, for no apparent reason. They may look like perfectly normal ordinary people. They may have personality problems or seem quite polite and friendly. If you're the sort of person who is drawn to them sexually, you may get involved in stormy relationships with a string of them. They may be your lover, your parent, your child, your friend. Why do they make you feel so strange?

And if you are one—and you know you are one, which is rare since most vampires are unconscious—your life may be hellish. People shy away from you and you can't figure out why. People treat you like an an outcast, and at the same time you are inexplicably drawn to them, almost against your will. You compulsively start trouble and can't understand where the impulse came from. You're hard to psychoanalyze. Maybe even your shrink winces when you walk in the door. Why did you have to be born like this? Or were you?

This book is not the kind of tirade against energy vampires that one sees occasionally occurring in other books on energy work. This book is for you—all of you—all vampires and people who love, honor, and struggle with them. It's for those of you who are not afraid to struggle and keep struggling, to the end of your days if necessary. It's a book about magic, and spirituality, and ethics. It's a book about discipline and hard work. If that last concept offended or frightened you, you'd best close this book right now, because it's only going to get worse.

Still with me? Good. Our first thorny problem is definition. What is this psychic vampire thing anyway, and why did I use the word "vampire"? It conjures up budget Hollywood movies and Count Chocula, or bad novels with people running around staking large-fanged undead fiends, or maybe listless angst-ridden teenagers with black lipstick dancing lethargically in darkened clubs to static-filled music.

I use the word because I think it's relevant. The concept of the vampire is universal. There's hardly a culture around who doesn't have some kind of vampiric figure in its folkloric mythos. Recently, in the last hundred years in Western culture, the world folklore has become combined, stratified, and given new symbolism. What was once gruesome is now subtly (and sometimes blatantly) sexual. What was terrifying is now titillating. When you say the word "vampire" now, a very specific image leaps into the Western conscious mind, something assembled and honed by authors and filmmakers.

But where did this concept come from originally? What is it about the concept of a human-looking but somehow inhuman predator that feeds on its "own" kind that fascinates us? Vampiric figures come in all sizes and shapes, from the Malaysian penanggalen which consists solely of a woman's head and intestines flying through the air to the Thai vampire who feeds on feces, not blood. Vampires all seem to want the same thing: some kind of human "life force" or vitality that they themselves lack, usually via some kind of human bodily fluid. They achieve this by either violence or stealth, or occasionally hypnotic seduction. Without it, they are at best weak and unhealthy, and at worst die. They can change their shape and use deception to get what they want, and are frequently associated with something spiritually dark and possibly evil.

All these characteristics are found to one extent or another in many energy vampires. (Don't jump to conclusions about that last quality. I neither believe that vampires are inherently evil nor that what we perceive as "dark" is always negative.) I use that word "vampire" precisely because it is loaded with connotations, just as many modern-day Neo-Pagans use the word "witch" in spite of centuries of bad press. Besides, we will get called by this term anyway, whether we like it or not. Mincing words and playing with euphemisms will simply imply a certain level of dishonesty and subterfuge, something which we are already associated with in the public mind. This book has been written to promote openness about this condition, not obscure it.

So what is this mysterious condition, anyway? Well, first you have to accept that there is such a thing as "life force". It runs through all things, but does not belong to them. As it runs through them, it takes on their vibrations (which is a fancy word for "thing-ness" or self-ness; tree energy is "tree-ness", human energy "human-ness", etc.) and is personalized by their essences. It is called, in different cultures, mana, prana, huna, ond, chi, ki, and by many other names. Some people can see it, and report that it flows in streams, webs, waves, like water, like electricity. It can come in AC/DC versions, it can polarize, it can depolarize. It comes in a million different flavors. It is what sustains us all.

In the past few decades, many different energy healing systems have come in from other parts of the world that specialize in working with various kinds of this life force—Reiki, Ch'i Gong, and other such traditions. Martial arts dojos may also stress this concept, especially when describing how the energy flows in a body making the correct move as opposed to a body that is awkward. This has brought the concept of prana into the American marketplace of ideas, although there are still quite a few skeptics. Magic workers—Neo-Pagans, Wiccans, magicians—have been working with it for some time, of course.

Human beings can get this energy from a number of places. When you were in the womb, it was your mother's energy field that fed you. As a post-birth human, you can get it from the earth, the air, other planes of existence, or wherever you like. You don't think about this, any more than you think about breathing. Probably less, too, since it's a lot easier for your nasal passages to be stopped than your prana circuits.

As you take in the prana from the whatever, your psychic circuits alter and transform it into something you can use (human-flavored energy) just as your digestive system breaks down and converts food into something you can use. Now imagine that you were born without a GI tract. In order to be nourished, you'd have to have your nutrients mainlined into your veins. You couldn't do this yourself, especially as a child; your feeding would be dependent on others for the rest of your life.

A primary—or "born that way"—energy vampire is just like that; born without the conversion circuits necessary to transform outside energy into human psychic nourishment. They are dependent on already converted energy to survive in good health. The only source of this is, of course, other living things—especially human beings.

(Disclaimer: I chose the terms "primary" and "secondary" vampires because they made sense to me, and accurately described what I saw in those around me who were psychic vampires. They are not numbered as to rank, power, worth, strength, difficulty, or general coolness. They are ranked in the order that the feeding talent is evident; primary vampires come with it already in place and functioning; secondary vampires acquire it through various means. Primary vampires are also somewhat more specialized and less versatile than secondary vampires. Obviously, you can't please everyone, and some people will disagree with these labels. I expect that, it's life. Perhaps someday in the future there will be enough research done to come up with a more accurate system of terminology, but right now that doesn't exist. Caveat emptor.)

I've been a psychic vampire all of my life. My daughter is one, and so are other relations who I won't mention for the sake of their privacy. It runs in my family, which makes me see it as something genetic. It's not unusual for specific psychic gifts to run in along bloodlines; I've come across many families where the "second sight" or telepathy or some other gift was the passed-down, barely-spoken-of inheritance coming from generation to generation. I don't see this as any different or any less genetically determined than my blond hair or learning disabilities or endocrine disorders that I see reflected in my parents. My daughter was watched throughout the second half of her gestation by an entire magical study group. At about the seventh month her vampiric tendencies were noticed by members who laid hands on her mother's belly. I consider this living proof—primary vampires are born, not made.

I'm not the only family of vampires I've met, either. Some were unconscious and at least one was very aware of what they were doing; the vampire father singled out the only vampire child—his eldest daughter—and taught her some of the techniques and dangers early on. The other children were told not to bother; this had nothing to do with them. In some families, certain gifts seem to run along with the vampire talents—always gifts that hinge on the ability to move energy around, such as weather-witching, poltergeisting, and shapeshifting of one kind or another.

Some primary vampires seem to come out of nowhere, in the sense that there is no one in their family with this gift. This may seem to put the lie to this theory, but of course we have to remember that we don't know enough to figure out if this is a dominant or recessive trait, or if it skips several generations, or if it is found as one of a bundle of traits that "stick together" genetically, and not all are expressed in every member of the family. More research needs to be done on this trait and its family inheritance.

You don't have to be born a vampire in order to move energy around from one human being to another, though. Sucking energy out of someone else—and putting it back—is a basic shamanic "trick", one of the techniques that a skilled energy worker learns as a matter of course. Every psychic healer worth their salt, whether they practice Reiki, ch'i gong, or something entirely different, has learned to do this at least to some extent. Almost any human being can be trained to do it, and many learn on their own.

Secondary vampires (another term I've coined) are a different matter entirely from primary vampires. It is quite possible to learn to be a vampire, even if you aren't one. It does take a good bit of work and effort for people who aren't used to it, for whom it isn't a natural thing, but it happens. Usually it happens to people whose natural energy gets exceptionally low, perhaps through illness, trauma, or addictions. If they are starving, so to speak, and have nowhere else to go, they may turn to energy vampirism in desperation, the way starving stranded pioneers in the Donner Pass turned to cannibalism to stay alive. I've noticed unconscious secondary vampirism occurring most often in people who are suffering from a chronic illness, such as CFIDS, fibromyalgia, genetic childhood diseases, or something else that is long and debilitating.

Another way to become a secondary vampire is to have a rotten childhood. Too much draining stress on a child can trigger them into reaching out to replenish it from the people around them. Secondary vampires can develop as early as four or five, if they are naturally psychically sensitive and they live in a sufficiently hellish environment. The most typical time for such a talent to be "picked up", however, seems to be around or just before puberty.

Most of these folks generally do it subconsciously, instinctively, and won't be consciously aware that they're doing it. Others may do it deliberately, for a variety of reasons. For one thing, energy sharing can feel very good, especially among (for example) lovers who trust each other. It can lend a thrill to sex, and it can also just feel good in a nonsexual situation. Some secondary vampires get that way because it becomes a fetish for them, or just a fun activity that they like to combine with their sex lives. They can even get psychologically hooked on the positive energy- sucking experience, and it can feel like an addiction to them.

There's another reason that someone may develop into a secondary vampire. Many an unethical mage has discovered that psychic vampirism is a good source of cheap-and-easy energy for magical workings, whether it is consensual or not. People such as this often keep a stable of people (or one poor stressed-out lover) to consciously use as ritual fodder for their workings. The feeders in general can be giving it out under informed consent, or not.

In the vampire communities (discussed in the chapter of that name), people often differentiate between a purely psychic vampire who draws off a living aura but does not break skin, and a "sanguinarian" vampire, who drinks the blood of their donor. It's the most uncomfortable part of thinking about vampires; after all, the legendary stereotype was of a creature who sucked people's blood out. Although it is controversial, I do address sanguinarian vampires in the chapter "The Blood Is The Life", because I believe, after many years of living and experimenting while being a vampire, that many sanguinarian vampires are actually psychic vampires who have figured out that fresh blood is glowing with high-density prana, and prefer the large, concentrated dose. Others, of course, indulge in this practice for other quite different reasons, and therefore are not germane to the span of this book. The practice of blood-drinking may horrify and disgust some people, but since a sizeable portion of conscious vampires actually do it, it would be hypocritical of me not to address it, and its attendant safety issues.

We psivamps have a bad rep, and frequently we deserve it, especially primary vampires. A vampire with no regular feeding source has a limited number of options for gathering energy: sex, physical affection, and causing intense emotions in others. Since vampire children find out fast that the latter can be accomplished with anyone from your parents to the grocery clerk, we learn the classic "provocative behavior" patterns at an early age. We learn to provoke arguments, stormy scenes, sexual frustration, tears, fears, or even violence from others, or manipulate everyone else while we look on and feed. "Let's you and him fight" was probably invented by a vampire.

Feeling hungry? Rile up your lover. Cling to a friend. Flirt with that guy who you know likes you, although you have no intention of actually delivering the goods. Argue about abortion rights with someone who has very strong feelings about the subject. Get someone to fall in unrequited love with you. Strip naked and let yourself be admired. Are you inspiring negative emotions? Possibly ... but hey, they're emotions, and you're hungry. I'm not pointing fingers. I've done it. Who am I to cast stones? It's easy, and when you can't get real blood or prana, it's like a bag of nachos when you can't get up the gumption to cook dinner. I can't say I'm completely 'sober' or in 'recovery' either. I am one of the most demanding, greedy, insecure people I know. However, being aware of the problem helps me to try to manage it.

–Sarah Dorrance, vampire

The problem is that since a primary vampire's been doing this sort of thing since before they could reason, they may well still be unconscious of it later, in adulthood. Not only are they unaware of why they do what they do, it never occurs to most of them to question it. I'd say that 90% of psivamps are operating on sheer habit and will react unbelievingly—and defensively—if you try to tell them what they're doing. This is not to say that the problem is hopeless, just tricky.

The stereotype of the vampire as thin, pale, and Byronic is a pretty inaccurate thing to go by. In fact, vampires are often overweight, because they attempt to compensate for their feelings of low energy and hunger by eating too much real food, which not only doesn't help but can compound the problem by physically slowing them down. It may help to give you perspective to imagine this: Instead of thinking of "vampire" as someone tall, dark, and romantic, think of Aunt Edna. Aunt Edna has a room temperature IQ, wears stained housedresses, and watches soaps. She has low-to-oblivious social skills, buttonholes anyone she can with long, boring conversations, and doesn't seem to mind that her victims are uncomfortable and trying hard to find an excuse to leave. In fact, this only seems to energize her. When you finally get away from her, you feel limp and drained. She has long since harangued her husband to death, and her children avoid her and are all in therapy or prison.

Aunt Edna doesn't really exist. I made her up, as a composite of the worst "average" unconscious vampires that I know. This book is also for the Aunt Ednas of the world, just as much as for the more conventionally attractive vampires, so that she can figure out why she does the things she's driven to do, and why all those nice people avoid her like the plague.

There are no specific physical markers with regard to being a vampire; no hair growing in the palm of the hand, or weird hairlines, or strange teeth. Sorry. I've seen vampires of all stripes in every size, shape, color, and gender. However, they might actually be rather pasty if they're nocturnal. We do have a tendency to being creatures of the night when we're ill-fed; as far as I can tell this has less to do with an allergy to sunlight and more to do with the fact that low-energy people's circadian rhythms are often severely off cycle. We may be insomniac for a long stretch and then sleep for two days. I know for myself that when I'm well-fed and energized, I'm more diurnal than when I'm "down".

By their actions shall ye know them, not their looks. The combination of provocative behavior patterns and the "drained" feeling of everyone around them is a good sign of the presence of a hungry vampire; one whose energy is low. A well-fed vampire may be calm, centered and charming, but one on overload—and it is possible to get overloaded and take too much—may be either grouchy and depressed or hyperactive and maniacally cheerful. Because of our energy swings, our moodiness is legendary, and we are called such words as intense, overwhelming, controlling, manipulative. One vampire characterizes herself as an "event horizon" when she is hungry, and tries hard to stay well-fed and avoid people when she is low-energy.

One trait that most of us do learn is something I've heard referred to as the "malocchio"—the evil eye. This is the ability to stare at someone and force our will onto them, if only for a second or a tiny bit. We learn how to do this, again, because it's necessary; it gets that little bit of energy and attention out of someone when it's most needed in our childhoods. No matter how repulsive many of us may look or act, we can throw that magnetic glance for just long enough to make you focus on us, and maybe long enough to make you interested. It's the built-in hypnotic talent of the predator.

Although there aren't specific physical markers that can be used across the board to identify any and all psychic vampires, if you can see into the astral, primary vampires are somewhat easier to pick out. Our auras tend to terminate in fringes of what many people describe as "tendrils" or "tentacles", depending on whether they are thread-fine or somewhat larger. (Those of us who are conscious can manipulate the size and length.) Those tendrils wave through the air like arms of a sea anemone, brushing up against other people's auras and "tasting" them. That's what makes people's auras contract and their skin crawl. When we feed, we do it through those tendrils, whether we are aware of it or not.

Some secondary vampires learn to grow tendrils, but it's not their native shape; they can extrude them and pull them back into the undifferentiated mass of their aura. They can also feed through other means. Other than that, there are few astral clues that are accurate for all vampires. Our auras vary in color and size, as do our bodies. We may have many different totemic shapes and animal affinities, not just bats and wolves as the popular literature might suggest. Predator totems do abound, but so, surprisingly, do scavenger totems, being that our nature partakes of both hunter and scavenger, and in many ways, psychic carrion-eater.

Many vampires are actually quite amoral about destroying people and discarding them. Like a shark or a mosquito, they exist only to feed and move on. They seem to feel that they have no room to spare in their lives for ethics; that morals would only threaten their survival. I tend to refer to this as "blender consciousness". What all vampires need to learn is that there is life beyond blender consciousness. It may not be an easy path, but it is a clean one.

Why bother with being an ethical psychic vampire? After all, you can't be arrested for doing the opposite. This, of course, is something that is up to each person, but I do believe in karma—in the sense that what you do does come back to you, sooner or later. What we put out, we get back, and so it's only sensible to be careful what you do. There's also the fact that I've seen far too many lonely and despised vampires out there. No matter how cool you think you are now, sooner or later you are going to get old and unattractive—unless you plan to die young and nasty and amoral while you can still charm people, in which case maybe you should do us all a favor and get it over with. Naw, that's mean of me, and unworthy, and I take it back. If I've learned nothing else, I've learned that every life is valuable, no matter how it looks on the surface.

My point—and I am pleading for understanding here—is that sooner or later we run out of looks, and tricks, and charm, and victims. It's better to have friends who like us enough to stick around. It's better for our own self-interest, too; being a user can wear away your soul. It gives one more power to have faith in one's own Word and one's own honor; to have enough self- worth to stand without guilt in the face of accusation. Remember, Bonnie and Clyde notwithstanding, banks always have more money than thieves.

2
Anger, Fear, Pain, and Sex: Learning Control

Just because one needs something does not mean that one has the right to make others miserable to get it. We all need food, but we don't knock someone over the head in the grocery store and steal their groceries ... or rather, if we were to do so, we would face consequences. There are consequences for the unethical stealing of energy as well. No matter how deft you think you are, when you're hungry, you're not that deft, and people will figure it out eventually if only on a subconscious level. At the very least, you'll end up disliked and friendless and alone, and that equals hungry.

When I was a beginning Pagan in my first coven during my teens (a coven consisting mostly of other teen novices), they were unprepared for the chaos I could wreak. They talked about how "drained" I made them feel, how they frequently recoiled when I came near, how my presence made their skin crawl for no reason they could pin down. (As I've said before, the skin prickling is a telltale sensation as one's aura retracts in reaction to being brushed by the sucking vortex of a vampire's aura.) Me, I was bewildered, felt helpless, and was angry at the lot of them. I also sabotaged more magical workings than I can count by "eating" the cone of power, which did not go over well with my coven mates. (For the record, it is unethical to eat the energy that people have raised for other purposes without their permission. Period.) Years later an experienced witch took me aside and explained to me what she saw in my aura; what she had identified me as being. I knew the moment she said it that it was true, but in my anger I reacted first with denial, and then with despair. What could I do? "Don't do it" was not an option. She had no answer. My own answers have been long and tortuous in coming.

LESSON # 1: Awareness. Become completely aware of your level of pranic energy and how it affects your behavior *at all times*. Your stomach tells you when it's hungry; learn to monitor yourself psychically as well. Enlist your friends, if you have any left. Have them tell you when you're resorting to provocative behavior patterns and ask how your energy is. Don't yell at them when they do it, either. This is a difficult discipline, especially in the face of denial and ingrained bad habits, and it may take years to get used to it. Still, the people around you may have a clearer view than you yourself when it comes to figuring out when you're doing it again. After all, you've been doing it for so long that it's second nature, an old and familiar habit.

You do have the right to ask them to tell you in a certain way. Decide what will be least likely to elicit a defensive response from you, and then be good about it. Figuring this out is your responsibility. Around here it's something like, "Are you hungry, hon?" said in a sympathetic and not accusing tone. However, remember that this is done to help you calibrate, and is not necessarily an offer to feed you. When they tell you that your hunger is showing, it's also your responsibility to back off, take several deep breaths, and try to decide rationally A) if they're right, or just misinterpreting your behavior, and B) what you're going to do about it. Don't be too quick to dismiss their observations; if you are hungry, it's in your best interest to fix the problem if possible.

I've actually noticed that a quite a few vampires have blood sugar problems on top of their other issues; often these are ones who have endured many years of prana deprivation. I have theorized that possibly disorders like hypoglycemia or diabetes may have been triggered by forcibly ignoring their energy needs for years, and along the way learning to tune out their physical food·needs as well, so that they starved or binged with food similar to their prana consumption. There's also the fact that the astral and physical bodies are linked together and affect each other, and doing a binge/starve pattern with one can impact the other similarly. At any rate, a vampire who is learning to care for his/her prana needs may also need to listen to his/her physical needs as well, and this may well be a new thing as the prana craving may actually have been drowning out the bodily needs for some time.

Exercise A: *Keep a journal. Each day, write down whether you are having feelings of: Nervousness. Twitchiness. Vague hunger that is not fulfilled by food. Clinginess. Irritability. Attempts to argue with or provoke others. Frustration and complaining over small things. Other behaviors that you know are endemic to you when you're prana-hungry.*

All of these things could possibly have other causes, of course, but you know yourself, or you should. The point of this exercise is to isolate the patterns that you fall into, and to figure out your limits—how long you can go before needing to feed, how long you can go before needing to feed to the point where it interferes with your functioning, how much is the minimum needed the keep going, and what works best.

Try going without for as long as you can stand, and write down your passing feelings. When you feed, record the circumstances, and how satisfied you did or didn't feel afterwards. If you're taking from a donor of some sort, ask them how much prana they think you actually took, and compare that to how much you think you got. When you've kept the journal for a couple of months, make a flow-chart and look at it. That's your pattern. Is it the pattern you want, or should you be working to do something differently?

Exercise B: *Make a list of all the different ways you get prana. List them in order of amount. Now relist them in order of quality. Now cross off anything that's unethical. Now make a new list of possible new prana sources for when you're in a pinch. Try them and add them to the first two lists.*

Next is the problem of ethical feeding. Whether you intend it or not, feeding off others to the point of their feeling drained without their consent is doing harm. Vampires should learn to shield before they learn to do anything else, for the protection of others as much as themselves. They must also learn ethical ways to get what they need.

There are different kinds of feeding—ambient feeding, contact feeding, and deep feeding. Ambient or "light" feeding can be done across a room, and involves feeding on the prana thrown off naturally in varied amounts depending on the subject's health and emotional state.

Physical contact is not necessary but can provide a better focus. Some performers, politicians, and other celebrities have learned to do this from shaking hands with adoring fans. In tiny doses, with no attempt to induce negative emotions, it doesn't seem to hurt anyone. The problem is that many vampires usually need more than tiny doses. Michelle writes: "I can get by on the ambient energy produced by large groups of people, but this is like bread and water for me. It keeps me going, but just barely. I prefer to feed directly from a steady partner."

When vampires venture out to lightfeed, they generally end up in places like loud concerts with lots of people screaming. I know quite a few vampire musicians who get some of what they need from the energy they can manipulate out of a crowd; I've done it myself. After all, performance is just consensual manipulation; people go there expecting the performer to "make" them have a good time. I've also met vampire teachers who lecture students and get them to respond— they're often the "better" teachers, not the ones who put you to sleep; if you're asleep, you're no good to them.

If they're not the terribly introverted types, vampires like jobs where they get to shake hands and make one-on-one contact with people; to "make" them feel a certain way. We grow up feeling like we need to control people, and often we have big control issues. It's not easy for us to let go of the people in our life and let them do what they want, because on some primitive level we see our food walking out the door when we that happens.

Contact feeding is a closer form of light feeding that involves skimming random loose energy off of the top of someone's aura. The aura of a healthy person who is not strongly shielded will constantly give off a faint cloud of energy, like the edge of an atmosphere. You can get slightly (or not so slightly) more energy from someone this way than you can from across the room. It's generally a one-on-one proposition rather than something you do in a group, and it may require some form of light touching, or at least being close enough to touch their aura. This also doesn't technically harm the person who's giving it off, because it's like you breathing their exhaled air; they don't need it and weren't going to reuse it. Contact feeding is a good technique to use for friends who are wiling to be your donor, but with whom you are not intimate.

The problem with contact feeding is that sometimes people can feel it. If they don't know what's going on, they may react to you in strange ways. They may find you suddenly very creepy or disturbing, or feel oddly violated by your presence. This is why I don't recommend doing it without letting people know first. You may think that you can get away with it, and perhaps if the other person isn't very psychically aware, they won't be conscious of what you're doing. However, they may well be unconsciously aware that something about you makes their skin crawl, and you might not want to get the kind of reputation that implies "vaguely disgusting molester-type".

Deep feeding is dipping directly into the energy flows of another to feed. It is a definite physical sensation—one feeder calls it "a pulling on my spine". Close physical contact is necessary. One deep feed can replace days of light feeding. Deep feeding is the first sort of feeding, learned in the womb by primary vampires who draw off their mother while gestating and then by the adults that pick them up and carry them around. Many forget how to do it and have to relearn it; they usually rediscover it through sex.

One problem with deep feeding is that is does create psychic bonds between the vampire and the donor, especially if it happens repeatedly. I wouldn't recommend it to two people unless they are willing to have that kind of close bond, which can become strongly empathic. Deep feeding is incredibly intimate (see the comments in the chapter *The Vampire Lover)*. It can also make people obsessed with each other, a condition that can be mistaken for falling in love. If only one shares this feeling, you can get a stalker problem. I've seen stalking issues on both the vampire side and the donor side. This is not something to do casually, or with anyone you can't imagine wanting to be bound to for a long time.

If you're a primary vampire who's been living by ambient and contact feeding for all of your born life, and you want to relearn how to deep feed, that will depend on how aware you are of your energy body and of moving energy in general. To start out, find a willing donor who fits the above emotional criteria. Ideally, you should find one who is pretty aware of their own aura and astral body and energy level, but if you have to make do with someone who is willing and eager but untrained, take special care. You might want to find someone else who moves energy, like a Reiki or Ch'i-Gong worker, standing by to help them out if you go overboard and they need replenishing.

Have your donor relax, and run your hands over them. Let the tendrils of your aura brush the edge of theirs. Ask them how they feel. If the sensation makes them uncomfortable, tell them that you're brushing their aura, and ask if they want to stop. (At any point, if they want you to stop, you should. This should never turn into a rape.) Now place your hands of their body, and touch their skin, and again ask if they want you to stop. You might want them to give a running commentary of their feelings and sensations.

Now sink your tendrils in past their skin. Let the tendrils float inside their body like seaweed waving in the ocean. At this point, you can feed a little. Inhale long and slow, while drawing the energy into you. It's one of the fundamentals of yogic breathing; a conscious, focused inhalation moves energy, while the exhalation allows you to rest. Keep breathing deeply, but not so hard that you hyperventilate. On each inhale, bring the energy into you through your tendrils and into the core of your body.

Remember that you can take a lot more prana a lot faster with this method. If neither you nor your donor has done this before, go slow. It's best to start counting breaths as soon as you start feeling the prana move into your body. Keep going for the space of ten more breaths, and then force yourself to stop. Move away from them physically to keep yourself from reflexively feeding further—cuddling and body contact is nice, but the physical boundaries between your body and theirs need to be reestablished first. Ask them how it went; have them sit up and move around and find out if they feel lethargic, or wiped out; find out how aware they were of the process and how it felt to them. Find out if the amount that you think you took has any relation to the amount that they perceived you having taken. If you took too much, do aftercare for them and next time don't go further than five breaths.

Be warned that you may have some odd symptoms afterwards. You may feel giggly and lightheaded, you may feel hyperactive, you may feel lethargic yourself and just want to lay around and "digest", as it were. I tend toward the "high" feeling myself, as if I'd done drugs. It can make me less than empathically sympathetic toward a donor in trouble, and I have to watch out for that.

Although light feeding generally doesn't hurt anyone as long as you didn't provoke bad emotions in order to get it, deep feeding can have adverse effects on the wrong people. Individuals who should be avoided as prana donors are:

1. Children. Just don't do it. Although they seem like inexhaustible bouncing balls of energy, they need every ounce of it for growth. Children don't always have the defenses to be able to say no; as with sexual activity, no child can legitimately consent to such a thing. The relationship of vampire/donor should be that of adult equals, so that no one is pushed beyond their boundaries.

2. Elderly people; they can be easily exhausted and their reserves are low.

3. People who are suffering from physical illness. Check first. They may have a "hidden" illness that is triggered by stress, which feeding can become. Even someone who is starting to come down with a "bug" can be depleted enough by a feeding that the germ overpowers the immune system that would normally have thrown it off.

4. Pregnant women. Their energy is tied up with making a baby. Leave it alone.

5. Mentally ill individuals. This is a tricky area. On the one hand, feeding can disturb a barely balanced mind and push it over the edge;

this goes especially for frequent feedings. Someone with a mental illness cannot always fully consent; they may react violently, or even after having consented, freak out and try to harm the vampire in question. I've found this to be especially difficult with people who suffer from Multiple Personality Disorder; the main "alter" may consent, but once the feeding starts, other "alters" may feel threatened and lash out. This can be both frustrating and dangerous for a vampire who is only trying to do the right thing.

On the other hand, there are quite a few professional vampires out there in the mental health field who do a great deal of good for clients with mental illnesses. The difference is that they have been trained to work with unbalanced individuals, and I strongly suggest that vampires should avoid people with a recent history of mental illness unless that have acquired some sort of training in the mental health field. It's a fine thing to be able to integrate one's ability to pull energy with one's knowledge of the mind, but one had better get well grounded in the mind's intricacies first. A pop book on how to figure people out does not count.

This brings us to another issue. Human energy doesn't all look—or taste—alike. It comes out of a human being stained, if you will, by that human being's nature and personality and aura, and also by whatever emotions that human being was experiencing at the time. Some energies taste better than others, and taste different to different types of vampires. This is one of the areas, in fact, where primary and secondary vampires diverge the most. Secondary vampires are out for the energy itself, and they either aren't picky about its flavor or they tend to prefer such "tastes" as sex, appreciation, approval, joy, happiness, excitement, and other positive flavors that you'd think would be the most likely candidates for the energy hunter.

Primary vampires are different. It's as if we have our circuits in backwards, almost. The energies that are the most attractive to us are, in brief, anger, fear, and pain, with sexual ecstasy a close fourth and occasionally even first. The more intense (and sometimes the nastier) the emotion, the more we are drawn to it, and the more we crave it from others on some level. This is why, if we're unconscious or amoral, we start fights, frighten people, tease people, hurt people, and generally make them miserable. Their misery feeds us; we need it and want it. We can make do on joy, but it's anguish that we want.

This is one of the reasons that many modern energy workers (especially those obsessed with white light) feel strongly that being a psychic vampire is some sort of malfunction that can be healed with the right amount of effort, compassion, and lots of white light. They couldn't be more wrong. However, I believe that this misapprehension comes out of a basic unwillingness to believe that the Powers That Be would deliberately make someone this way. How, they ask, could this be a natural thing?

The answer to this question is the key to the karmic purpose of the primary vampire. I strongly believe that God/dess does not make junk, or mistakes, and that we have a crucial role in the psychic ecosystem. We are the equivalent of the carrion-eaters, the garbage disposals who get rid of all the negative filth that wounded people spew every day. In the real ecosystem, there are a number of species whose job it is to eat things that we humans would retch at, and without them, the world would be considerably less comfortable. However, in order to fill this niche, those creatures have to be built to digest what they eat. We mirror Nature, because we are part of Nature.

Although many animals in the physical ecosystem eat carrion— dogs, wolves, the Corvidae family of birds for whom I am named—the one creature who most closely resembles a primary psychic vampire in its niche form is the vulture. This bird has evolved to the point where it can eat nothing but rotting meat; feeding it a diet of fresh meat will cause it to become ill. Its head is bald (and thus aesthetically unappealing to us) so that it can stick its entire face into a rotting corpse and get to what's inside. Having held one once, I can assure you that they stink, and we humans make derogatory comments about them, especially because they do circle an area when they are waiting for something to die. However, even if we find them unpleasant, they do an important job that we should be grateful for, and it is our bias that flinches at their needs, not Nature's.

The image of the vulture isn't a very romantic one, but it is accurate. We are designed from before birth to seek out and "eat" negative energy, and we have a special talent that allows us to "digest" it unharmed. If anyone else—say, someone with training in psychic healing—pulls nasty, gunky, anger-fear-pain energy out of someone, it will take them a while to clean and convert it, assuming that they can even hold onto it at all without becoming ill. Most healers are advised by their teachers to let that energy pass out of them and into the Earth, the biggest cleanser of all. They are warned that holding onto it, or continually utilizing it, or even letting it pass through them frequently can result in that energy "staining" them as well, making them ill or off-balance or logy. Even if you are the type who likes the taste of it, too much of it on a regular basis can infect you with ongoing negativity.

Some primary vampires, on the other hand, can convert negative energy to clean energy in mere seconds, without even trying. These folks' auras are like filters, or ionizing lasers; they "vaporize" everything off—emotions, personality, taste, everything—and absorb the energy harmlessly. Some magical workers who deal in animal totems speak of "snake medicine", which is the ability to eat poison and transmute it into harmless water with the power of your own body. What primary vampires in general do to human energy is snake medicine on a psychic level, to one degree or another. We can take all your horrid stuff off your hands without harm to ourselves, because we are designed to digest it. We eat rot and thrive, because Nature needs carrion-eaters in every ecosystem. No matter how much pain is in you, I come away smiling.

One note, though: No matter how powerful a primary vampire you are, there are energies out there that you cannot digest, and that will make you ill. This is especially true for magicians who mess about with energies not native to this Earth and this plane. It's worth it for even primary vampires who are accustomed to eating anything with no ill effects to bother to learn psychic cleansing methods. Some of these are outlined in *The Urban Primitive*, which I put out with Tannin Schwartzstein (especially the second edition); some other useful ones can be found in *Basic Psychic Hygiene* by Sophie Reicher.

This doesn't mean that primary vampires can't "eat" positive energy. We can, and do, especially when it comes in large quantities, such as the adoration of a crowd when we perform. (Many vampires have found a career in performance or politics worthwhile, for obvious reasons.) However, positive energy is like oatmeal to a primary vampire. It's nutritious, but a little bland in large amounts. When I'm groggy in the morning, I like oatmeal, because it's inoffensive and easy to deal with. When I'm ill or weak, I sometimes like positive energy because it doesn't come with the emotional difficulties of negative energy. However, if you take me to a restaurant and give me a choice between oatmeal and a really good filet mignon with parmesan fettuccine, I'm going to ignore the oatmeal. The latter is more like what negative energy "smells" like to us, and we find it hard to resist.

On the one hand, this often puts us in a strange double bind. No sane person really likes to see people in pain, or angry, or suffering, or afraid, especially if we love them, but at the same time this is when people are most attractive to us. Obviously, this dual message can result in someone who goes terribly wrong; who becomes psychologically sadistic or manipulative or abusive. These sorts of vampires abound, and it would be foolish of me to deny it.

On the other hand, it can also result in someone who goes in the other direction. One of the most compassionate and caring therapists I know is a man who takes on the serious trauma victims that his colleagues find too difficult to handle—the rape victims, the sex abuse victims, the multiple personality disorder patients who must sometimes spend entire sessions sitting under his desk and weeping. He is also a primary vampire, and he takes everything they throw at him and absorbs it. Nothing they give him can upset him, and he takes their considerable pain off their shoulders, at least for that one session, and leaves them a little freer each time. Of course, he's getting paid twice—

once in money and once in all that fear-energy—which is an excellent motivation for him to be patient with them. This sort of thing is what we're designed for; it's what Nature intended us to do.

In fact, one of the most popular professions for intellectual vampires is that of therapist, and we are often quite successful at it. It also guarantees us a steady supply of people showing up on our doorstep with negative energy to dump. Even less intellectual ones often become unofficial counselors; the sort of person who has distressed individuals showing up on their doorstep all the time, pouring out their woes, and coming away feeling better. We'll go further into how to carry out this work in the chapter "Healing The World".

Another problem with continual energy feeding is that if you feed off of one person for too long, you can start to absorb that person's traits through their energy. Although we can generally convert any one dose of negative energy to "clean" energy in record time, we aren't machines, and prolonged contact with one sort will stain. If their energy is "blue", and you take it regularly, pretty soon you'll start to be tinged with "blue" as well. This can be useful if you need "blue" energy in your life, and as such it is part of the shamanic technique bag of tricks. However, if you don't want to be that much like your lover, you'll have to be more careful. This is, obviously, a real problem for secondary vampires.

However, this brings us back to the central problem of How To Get Fed On a Regular Basis. There will be times when you don't have the emotional strength (or the time) to deal with someone's pain, and you just want a quick jolt of something fairly neutral that you don't have to work too hard to get. This is when it's good to have a network of friends and family and tribe who are aware of what you need and are willing to give it, at least in small amounts.

LESSON #2: Be nice to your friends and lovers! Tell them about your needs, and ask for help. This is the hardest part of all for any vampire, but it's the only truly clean way. You can do ambient feeding ethically without telling someone as long as you aren't provoking the emotions that create that energy. This is all right because ambient feeding collects the prana that everyone leaks more or less all the time, and does not deplete them. However, for deep feeding, you are going to have to ask. This requires coming clean about everything. It doesn't matter whether or not they believe you when you tell them, "Look, I'm a psychic vampire, and when I'm hungry I need to do such-and-such to you, and I promise not to take too much or hurt you," and so on. Even if they don't believe it, they have to have the chance to refuse. Give them the choice and respect it. If it makes them uncomfortable and they don't want to do it, back off and don't pressure them. Find someone else.

Don't put the burden all on one person. Learn the energy meridians in a human body (most vampires have an instinctive grasp of where these are anyway, if they think about it) and learn to deep feed—preferably through the skin because it's safer. Consent is the litmus test of an ethical situation, so always ask before any more than the lightest of feedings, and take no more than they are comfortable with. Good donors demand respect and consideration for their gift, so treat them well! And never go into any group magical working hungry; feed first or bow out. When you can ascertain your hunger, ask, and be fed willingly by people who are doing it because they like you, you are well on your way away from blender consciousness.

For purposes of jargon, many vampires refer to "donors" as people who occasionally consent to give a little prana to a hungry vampire friend, and "feeders" as full-time donors, usually lovers or partners of vampires. (Others may use "donors" for both types; it varies and there's no complete consensus.) An ethical vampire will be careful not to take too much at any one time; if the donor isn't feeling their best, they should be let alone in order to recoup. Taking a dangerous amount at one sitting will be evidenced by the following symptoms: The donor becomes very cold, and perhaps gets chills as if going into shock. They feel lightheaded, nauseated, and confused, and "off". They feel a desperate need to cling physically to the vampire; this is because their body is reacting to the fact that their aura is depleted of energy, and that energy is now mostly in the vampire's aura, and by clinging to them they are still in its circle. They may hyperventilate. If you can see their aura, it will be shallow—closer to their body than normal—and thin, and grayish. They may feel as if there are large holes in their aura—"leaks" through which still more energy is escaping. That may be true; it is possible to temporarily tear holes in someone's energy system through overfeeding.

These holes will heal in time—anywhere from a day to a week depending on the stamina of the individual—but they cause havoc with the donor's body, astral and physical, and can result in a lowered immune system while the aura is still leaking. (Although it's possible to make tears like this without breaking the skin—I've done it—the usual culprit of such accidents is making a cutting to get blood and letting too much come out.) I've heard of foolish vampires who'd read too much Anne Rice and told victims of this kind of incompetence that they were "being converted" to vampirism, and that this kind of weakness and shock was the "first sign" of their "dormant vampire tendencies coming forward". Balderdash, say I. Don't believe a word of it. It's only evidence that the vampire screwed up.

If you are the vampire who has just accidentally taken too much and put your feeder into shock, you have a responsibility to clean up your mess. Don't leave them alone. Stay with them, and give them physical contact—they'll feel most comfortable contained in your aura, until their own is a little better. Explain to them what has happened; take responsibility for it, even if it's embarrassing. If you can, feed a little of your own energy back into them. (Not all primary vampires are capable of outflow, and sometimes energy coming out of a primary vampire doesn't feel very good to another person, so this may or may not work. If you're a secondary vampire and you've screwed up in this way, give back as much as you can; you have no excuse.) If the person knows how to ground and center, help them to do so; if they don't, help them to visualize the hole sealing over, and perhaps walk them through a visualization about pulling energy up from the Earth, which is always forgiving.

If they need to drive home, check to see that they're well enough to do so before letting them walk out the door. If you need to drive them home, do it. If they need to spend the night, let them, if it's at all possible. Stay in physical contact with them as long as you can. Check on them over the next few days to make sure that they are recovering, and try to see that they get good nutrition during that time, as the body needs extra help to make sure that it won't be affected by the energy leaking. If they know how to ground and center, they should be doing it morning and night to help with their energy levels.

This isn't how a feeding should go, anyway. It should ideally proceed something like this: It is negotiated beforehand, including what method will be used, and both parties are consenting, and fairly sanguine about the matter. The donor should trust and feel comfortable with the vampire, and the vampire should do what he/she can to make the donor feel safe. The vampire proceeds with the feeding slowly, testing the waters. If there is resistance in the aura, if you feel the person trying to hold back or throw up shields, even though they have agreed to it, stop. If you force the issue, you could hurt them. It probably means that some part of their subconscious is not comfortable with this, and with you. Don't berate them or take it personally. People often have subconscious issues about trust, and you can't make them trust you. Explain the situation and back off. Don't make them feel like it's their fault.

If you don't feel resistance, feed just enough so that they will have no ill effects. This amount will vary from person to person, and it's best to go by trial and error, and err on the side of not enough rather than too much. Different people will react differently to a feeding. For some, it creates sexual arousal; for others, a feeling of well-being. For some, though, it may trigger feelings of violation, and they may not want you to continue. If your donor is becoming uncomfortable for any reason, they should be able to tell you clearly and have you instantly respect their request. They should not have to fight you off under any circumstances.

Afterwards, although they may feel tired or a little lethargic, they should not feel sick or unable to move. (Dealing with pain from illness is dealt with in another chapter.) They may feel a little cold, especially if they are prone to coldness in general, so throw a blanket around them, However, they shouldn't go into an attack of the shivers and shudders—that may mean that you took too much. Feed them nourishing physical food at this time, and let them rest. They've served you, and now you should serve them.

Exercise C: *With a willing volunteer, run your hands over someone's body, keeping them about half an inch away from the skin. Try to sense where the astral energy channels run. You'll find that they are close to the skin in such areas as the sides of the neck, the insides of the wrists and to a lesser extent, elbows; the insides of the thighs just on either side of the groin. If the volunteer is willing, draw the lines on them in chalk or lipstick so that you can see it in your mind.*

If the volunteer is willing to give up some of their prana, pull small bits of it from different areas. Which are easiest? Now try different techniques of drawing it out. First, sit across the room and see if you can reach them from where you are. Visualize your aura reaching out like tendrils to sink into theirs. Now sit next to them and do it. Now hold your hands a half-inch away again and try it. Now touch them and try it. Try breathing in when you bring the energy into you—that's a trick that many vampires work out for themselves. Inhale—feed; exhale, rest. I feel it like a hydraulic pump bringing the prana up into my core. Which techniques work for you and which don't? Ideally, your volunteer should be telling you at every point what they are feeling. If they start to get tired or fuzzy or lightheaded, stop and take it up again another day.

If you can, try this exercise with several different volunteers, so you can get a feel for different people's bodies and how they handle their prana. Some people's auras will resist you. Some people will find it so uncomfortable that they'll have to ask you to stop. If you can, figure out what that feels like to you, that involuntary psychic recoiling. Memorize it. Teach yourself to immediately pull back whenever you feel it, even from someone who's given you their verbal consent. Sometimes someone can consciously consent, but unconsciously dislike the idea. It's better not to force the issue.

For direct contact feeding, I generally use my hands. Touch is combined with breathing so that the breath becomes the real focus for drawing the energy into me, while the hands are the point of contact where the energy is drawn away from my partner. To an outside observer, my feeding probably looks a good deal like a Reiki attunement ... but of course, in Reiki, the hands are used to put energy into a person, while I use my hands to take energy out. With either hands or mouth, there are certain areas on the partner's body where it's easier to make a connection to their energy. The major chakras are significant points of contact, with the heart, solar plexus, and throat being the three which I prefer just for ease of accessibility. The minor points in the wrists and hands work well too. I tend to prefer the throat above all others because it doesn't require the partner to take their clothes off.

–Michelle

3
The Vampire Lover

I think that my life would have been much easier for me if my vampirism did not require me to rely upon other people for my health and well-being. It's quite a head-trip, really, coming to terms with the fact that your life requires you to take life from others. It's not like I'm killing the people I feed from, but there's no denying that I'm taking something vital away from them. They will eventually recover the energy I've taken, but in the meantime, they can be headachy and lethargic. Over the course of time, if I take too much too often, it seems to impact their immune system, and they get sick more frequently.

That can be a little scary. The ethical ramifications are profound. How can I, who strive to live my life selflessly, justify this need in me to take from people? There's no way you can vampirize someone completely selflessly. You know from the get-go that you're going to tire the other person out so you can feel alive and well. But there's a point where you just have to accept it and be selfish once in a while, or you'll drive yourself crazy with guilt and self-loathing. It wasn't easy for me, and I still have trouble justifying it sometimes. That's one of the main reasons I refuse to feed from anyone who is unwilling or unaware of what I'm doing. If they know what it will do to them, and they are still willing to do this for me anyway, I can accept it as a gift and not some onerous task I'm imposing on them.

–Michelle

The idea of having a vampire lover is pretty sexy to a lot of people. The reality may be somewhat less so. We vampires tend to be high-maintenance, sad to say, even those of us who are conscious and ethical. We want lots of attention, and I've never met a vampire who was happy with a lover or spouse who wasn't willing to be a prana donor, at least if they were monogamous. By definition, a vampire's lover ends up being part of their pantry, and often they don't have a lot of prana to give back. We can learn to give back in other ways, though.

There are many paths to a lover's heart; many ways to make yourself "worth the trouble".

Most vampires are highly sexed, or at least appear that way. Sexual energy tastes very good to vampires; it's the only positive type of prana among the top four "favorites". In fact, sexual energy seems to be the best-tasting positive energy to all primary vampires, and I've rarely met a secondary vampire who would turn it down either. If many vampires seem more blatantly sexual than average, it may be less about libido and more about hunger. Conscious vampires often learn to be good lovers in the physical sense, as it's more useful to them for their partners to be intensely aroused for long periods of time, and have strong orgasms that they can then "eat".

Feeding can trigger sexual arousal in some people, although that's by no means common to all. (In fact, the two most common knee-jerk reactions to being the subject of deep feeding are either a strong feeling of violation, or sexual arousal—and sometimes both at once, which can be confusing for the donor.) It may be due to the shifting of energy fields in the body of the donor, or the psychic intimacy of feeding, or perhaps the romance of the "vampire image". If feeding accompanies sex for any length of time, the donor can become conditioned to arousal through feeding whether or not they started out that way. For some, it can be an addiction, and if actual bloodletting is involved for any length of time, a fetish.

However, if you're a conscious vampire, do your lover/donors the courtesy of being clear and aboveboard with them about what you're doing, and let them have a say in it. Vampires whose lovers don't consciously know what's going on psychically in bed often find themselves shut off from sex when the lover simply feels low-energy and instinctively avoid intimacy with their hungry partner. The astral body does attempt to protect itself, in whatever way it can, and that may include shutting out a possible drain when there's not enough to go around. A lover who knows what's going on, and can talk about both his/her psychic needs and his/her lovers' needs can soften such rejections and create fewer excuses for an argument, which is often a desperate vampire's last resort.

Even cuddling with a vampire can be a psychically violating experience for some people, especially a primary vampire who does not have their "tendrils" under full control. It's natural for us, when we are being physically close and affectionate with someone, to want to sink our psychic tentacles into them, so to speak. If we're well fed, this won't necessarily even be to feed, but just to form that extra bond. For some people, especially those with strong shields and boundary issues (perhaps from years of abuse), this can feel creepy, even if only on an unconscious level. On the other hand, some lovers enjoy the intimacy of being subtly invaded, not just a mingling of auras but of astral body energy as well. One lover of a vampire commented that it was like being "extra cuddled".

> It is amazing to just be held by him. To be really held. Not just skin to skin, but to feel him wrapped around your lungs. To feel him twisted through your intestines. To feel him coiled tightly around your spine. To have a lover who can touch the inside of you as easily as he can touch the outside of you.
>
> –Joshua, lover and full-time donor

Some vampires also play with such games as S/M. Although the discussion of consenting S/M deserves (and has) its own books, and we have neither the time nor the space to diverge into it here, let me just say that if you are the vampire and the Top, and you are feeding as part of the negotiated scene, then feeding and how it is to be done should be part of the negotiation, and clearly consented to. It should go without saying that everything else should also be negotiated and consented to. Sex games in general are a good way to get your sexual energy mixed with that yummy fear energy without actually harming anyone. It's OK to play a one-man-or-woman haunted house for an appreciative audience. If you are the vampire and the bottom, be careful if you use a particularly "needy" and dependent scene persona as a way to get fed. That can be annoying to your top after awhile. Being a disobedient submissive in order to piss them off is also not a very good idea, unless that's negotiated beforehand.

> I suppose it would be appropriate to go on about how intense and wonderful the sex is, but that alone wouldn't give an accurate picture. The feeding does create an amazing intimacy, but anyone skilled at sex magic and energy movement could get the same effect in many different ways. I think the big difference is in the play of predator and prey. When he feeds, it isn't a mystic exercise or an attempt at emotional closeness, but a direct expression of his hunger. Perhaps it is terribly unenlightened of me, but I find the raw passion of it much more exciting than any lofty spiritual or emotional goals. It is thrilling that his natural instinctive response to me is to want to devour me. I don't think any non-vampire could match him in expressing that sort of passion.
>
> –Joshua

If you're going to be in non-casual relationships with your donors, you'd also better make yourself into someone worth being with. It's not unusual that vampires can be pretty insecure people; in fact, insecurity is a frequent hallmark of both primary and secondary vampires. Secondary vampires may even have taught themselves to prana-feed as a way to salve their own insecurity. Primary vampires may well have developed the insecurity due to the mixed messages of their childhood, and the unconscious worry about whether their "food" would abandon them; in that case it is the vampirism that created the insecurity, and not the other way around. However it came about, it can be irritating to the people that you will be depending on.

Although everyone gets a little insecure about being left, and nobody likes to be abandoned, vampires often get almost hysterically attached to a donor. Seeing not only your source of love and affection, but your food as well, walking out the door can trigger an instinctive desperate-predator response, often resulting in stalking, violent jealousy, and other undesirable situations. Sometimes these overreactions, occurring during a relationship in response to some imagined infidelity, can be the straw that breaks the camel's back and eventually forces the lover to leave, thereby becoming a self-fulfilling prophecy. A vampire involved in a breakup is an especially vulnerable person. If you're that vampire, breathe deeply, a lot. Try to understand that part of your obsessive feeling isn't so much a longing for the beloved as for what they represent, and try to sort out one feeling from the other. Go looking for other sources of food immediately; don't skulk around in your apartment starving and miserable. Once you've gotten yourself fed from another source, the semiconscious part of you that is responsible for your survival will shut up, and you'll be more able to work on letting go.

It's better than the kind of terrible scenes I've seen from some vampires and their exes, the kind that end up with restraining orders and jail time and long, drawn-out nastiness. Also, refrain from the kind of vengeful idea that since they left (and hurt) you, they're fair game for any energy you can get out of them, with or without their consent. That's petty and unworthy, and very bad karma. Grit your teeth and take the moral high ground, even if it hurts. The universe will be more likely to reward you with another, more appropriate, lover if you prove your worthiness rather than your maliciousness.

Another thing that I've seen not work is the vampire in search of the right lover to save them from their vampirism. Unless you are dating a minor deity, this isn't likely to happen; any more than a lover can save you from deafness, or diabetes, or Asperger's Syndrome, or having acne or thin, stringy hair. You're the only one who can do anything about your own vampirism. Of course, finding someone who is supportive and willing to help you through some of the problems can, indeed, feel like a godsend, but a partner can only do so much, and that only if you let them know what needs to be done, and let them make their own decisions as to whether they can handle it.

If you've mastered the art of vampire charm, you may actually get by for some time on that, but not forever. Don't make the mistake of thinking that you can charm and misdirect and manipulate your partner into not noticing bad vampiric behavior on your part. Not only is it Wrong, but sooner or later they will figure it out, and leave you. The first rule, of course, is that you should be explaining your situation as a psychic vampire to them as soon as things get serious. If you don't think they can handle the explanation, you shouldn't be dating them.

If you don't want to use the V-word at first, that's all right (although if you're a sanguinarian, it's pretty futile to avoid it), but choose some kind of clear, simple way to tell them. It's not fair to draw someone into a serious relationship and then spring this sort of thing on them when they're in too deep to extract themselves without pain. (It may seem like a clever thing to do if you're a desperate and amoral vampire, but it is, as I said, Wrong.) Be prepared to delineate what this will mean for them—what they can expect, what you need from them in terms of prana and attention and help with your energy discipline. Warn them that they will need to develop strong boundaries, and be aware of their energy levels. Give them permission to ask you if you're prana-hungry, even if you're irritable and pissy. Actually, especially if you're irritable and pissy. Learn to reply graciously and not defensively.

LESSON #3: Work on yourself. Try to get past those feelings, by whatever means necessary, before you drive your food sources away. Just being nice to them is a good thing, but eventually they will see through a mere mask of courtesy, and you may get tired of keeping them out in terror of them seeing what you're really like. You don't have to be perfect, but you shouldn't let yourself dissolve into a sucking maw of low self-esteem.

Sarah's Suggestions For Building Vampire Self-Esteem:

1. Give yourself attention every day. Gaze into the mirror and force yourself to admire yourself, even if it's one body part at a time. Let yourself believe that you are a beautiful and fascinating person. This isn't conceit; if you are truly dull and horrid, someone will poke a hole in your bubble soon enough. It's pampering. If you don't pamper yourself, you will demand that other people give it to you along with

their prana. This annoys them, which gets you lots of negative energy to feed from, but which also tends to make people around you feel mentally raped or at least harassed, and that drives away your food supply (to put it bluntly and crassly). So give yourself lots of positive attention when you feel like it. So what if it's five times a day? So what if it feels like pleasuring yourself (which I strongly endorse; why not indulge if you have the time and energy)? You don't just deserve it, you need it.

2. Don't be self-obsessed to the point of narcissistic paranoia, but do be introspective. Examine your feelings. When you feel an emotion, take a little while to think about why you feel it. When you feel blue or uncomfortable, examine the source of your pain. Try free-associating on paper, if that helps. Talk it over with a counselor or a friend, if possible. Think. A lot of attacks of insecurity and nastiness can be prevented by a little self-honesty. Don't bury your feelings; be honest with yourself about what they are, and try to examine why you feel that way, and think about various ways to make yourself feel better. Sometimes distractions help too.

3. Can you perform—music, dance, or drama? If so, do it! Getting the attention of a rapt audience gives you a strong buzz, and it has the advantage of taking small amounts of energy from a number of different people rather than taking large amounts of energy from one or two people.

4. Think about joining a support group, for anything you might be remotely involved with. Why? See #3. You can get group attention doing this.

5. Strike a healthy balance between needing others and being alone. You need to learn to be comfortable with aloneness, even if it makes you feel anxious or stressed to the max. Otherwise, you'll send off "desperation" vibes when you socialize that scare away your donors. Nobody likes a hungry, desperate vampire. A healthy, well-fed vampire is very lovable and inspires intrigue and fascination. To get fed, you have to seem like you are taken care of, even if you are not.

6. Take personality quizzes. I've found that it's an easy and mesmerizing form of self-love. It also sometimes tells you something you don't already know about yourself, although learning stuff that you already know is even better because it gives you what you crave emotionally: self-validation. It reassures you that, yes, you are real, you are you, and you are utterly fascinating, really. Believe it or not, everybody needs to believe that; it's not just you, although you have an added reason for needing self-validation.

7. Take care of your health. Bad health makes you hungrier and will make you drain people a lot more. *(See the chapter on Bodies.)*

8. When you do get positive attention, give it back. That way you'll keep getting more positive attention. *(Raven's note: Remember that you do not have to eke out your precious prana to smile, say a kind word, look attentive, compliment someone, carry on a pleasant conversation, or hand somebody the pretzel dish. Just because you associate attention with feeding doesn't mean that everyone else does. Don't fall into the trap of being stingy with your attention because you secretly assume that everyone else is a vampire like you.)*

9. Never chase after a subject who is trying to distance themselves from you. Ever. Only feed from people who are eager and willing. It's not just ethics; it's also good common sense, as cultivating the willing gets you a lot more energy and keeps you better fed, and it's also self-esteem. It's hard on your soul to be constantly treated like a monster to be escaped from.

10. Be open and honest. People hate having to guess whether or not that strange vibe they get from you is really because you're sapping them of energy, or if they're just paranoid. If you say, "I'm hungry and I need some more attention," honestly and openly, they may feel relieved enough to actually humor you.

Another way in which we vampires are irritating to our lovers is our love of drama and intensity. It's not just that we find *sturm und drang* tasty in a lover. After years of chasing it around, we tend to absorb the behavior as well. Some of us overreact to things, or make wide, sweeping melodramatic gestures and statements. (There are also, of course, quiet and self- contained vampires who don't need to do this. It may have a lot to do with how well-fed you were in your early life.) Sometimes it becomes a habit with us, and it's hard to stop.

We are also drawn to books and movies that are dramatic or scary, for similar reasons. I call this the catnip response, after watching my cat roll around for months with a toy ball that all the catnip had long since fallen out of. There was no way for her to get high off of the tiny whiff that was left, but she lay on the floor and chewed it anyway, because she remembered that it had once made her high in the past. Scary movies and angst-ridden books give us no actual prana, but they remind us subconsciously of things that do, and so we like them. We may actually convince ourselves that we are getting something more than a memory stroke out of them. One can tell the unconscious hungry vampire over the Internet; he's the one yelling and flaming with others. He can't get prana over the Internet from unsuspecting strangers, although he may claim that he can. It's more about force of habit and the catnip response. He's so used to dealing with people this way, and is so drawn to conflict, that he'll do it without thinking. Starting fights over the Internet is like eating iceberg lettuce; the fact that you are chewing and swallowing seems familiar, but you get no nourishment out of it.

Lovers of vampires either love or hate the melodrama. Some are drawn to it because they find it exciting or interesting; others can feel pushed around by their vampire's control issues (Every vampire has control issues, in varying stages of severity.) A vampire's partner has to learn to say, "That's enough. Let's calm down, take a few breaths, and see if the situation is really that bad." The vampire has to force themselves to listen to that, even if it goes against their habits.

People think of vampires as being the bully in the relationship, but there's another sort of vampire altogether—one who plays the victim. This vampire will pair up with a highly emotional person with little self-control, and then needle them into losing that self-control frequently. These vampires will even put up with battering if it means that they get fed with the partner's anger. They can also look like the victim, and hold the high moral ground, while they're subtly encouraging the raging partner. I am certainly not implying that all or even most battered, codependent spouses are actually psychic vampires, but this pattern does occur, especially for more introverted vampires who suffered through abusive childhoods. On some level, they may associate abuse with getting fed, and until they are conscious of this association and what it means, they will keep seeking out abusive lovers to feed on.

Still another negative pattern that unconscious vampires get into is that of wounded/healer. With this coupling, the (usually but not always a primary) vampire has gone far enough to learn how to relieve someone of their fears and pain by bleeding off that aching energy, and knows on some level that they feel good when they do it. They pair up with a traumatized person with lots of problems, and proceed to become their caretaker, giving them sympathy and "eating" their pain. At first, all is well, but the problem arises when the wounded partner starts to get closer to healing. If the vampire is unconscious, their survival mechanism will decide that it is in their own best interest to keep their partner a tasty wounded victim rather than a strong, healed human being. They will subtly find ways to sabotage the partner's confidence and healing process, encouraging them to self-pity and "victim consciousness", so that there will always be plenty of wounds for them to bind and "eat". If the "wounded" partner ever does get far enough along in their healing that they don't need the vampire's services, or if they pick up on what's going on, the relationship usually breaks up.

I've rarely met primary vampires who pair up with each other, although it does happen. Primary vampire energy can sometimes "taste bad" to people, including other vampires. On the other hand, it does have a quality all its own, one that is less nourishing than other human energies, but it can have a "speedy" or amphetamine-like effect. Some primary vampires who do feed off each other will enthuse about how energetic they feel afterwards, but that's more along the lines of someone claiming that speed gives one more energy than food, a statement that is both true and untrue. Occasionally, primary vampires will get addicted to the speedy feeling and prefer feeding off of each other, a situation which I have not found useful, so I can't describe it in detail. Some primary vampires claim that they can feed off of each other in a circle, passing the energy around, as it were, but one would think that new energy has got to come from somewhere. When this sort of thing happens, I suspect that one or more of them are getting energy from outside sources to bring in.

Primary vampires also tend to have instinctive violent reactions to anyone attempting to feed off of them. Any vampire/vampire relationship is going to have a certain amount of power struggle by its nature, but two primary vampires have to constantly fight the territorial predatory challenge urge. Sometimes we end up facing off like a pair of snarling carnivores, each unconsciously sure that the other is some kind of terrible threat that must be crushed. If we do manage to get past each others' trigger-happy boundaries, we can drain each other into a mutual state of depressed, snappish irritability in no time. I won't say that such a relationship couldn't endure, because Love can conquer all sorts of boundaries, but the individuals involved would probably have to be very aware, very patient, very rational, and have lots of other support people to feed them properly.

Secondary vampires can and do get into relationships with primary vampires, and with each other. Sometimes a donor-partner ends up being a secondary vampire through overdraining, and subsequently learns to reach out to others for energy in turn. Sometimes simply being the focus of such activity can teach them a lot about how to do it, and they can learn how useful and enjoyable it can be. With one primary and one secondary, the secondary still tends to end up being the donor more often than not, and it can feel one-sided. It may be that the only thing to do is to bring in more sources of energy to feed both parties. With two secondaries, the partners can take turns feeding each other, assuming that both are amenable and one isn't trying to dominate the other emotionally.

Sex with a vampire usually means feeding. It's almost impossible for us to resist; asking us not to feed during sex is like asking us to put food in our mouths but not swallow it. A well- trained, ethical vampire will be careful not to drain you. An unconscious or amoral vampire may take a lot. We usually have very strong sexual appetites—if only because sex is so bound up with food for us—with the exception of the manipulative vampire who has learned that withholding sex causes delicious frustration. (Delicious for her, anyway, unless she's a dominatrix with a masochistic partner.) When the sex frequency goes downhill, a vampire may become frightened and feel desperate, and push for more sex. The partner needs to work out ways to reassure them that it's only temporary, and they will be back.

The problem is that it's no fun to be wanted primarily as a food source. Smart people will sense, if only subconsciously, if that's the case, and they will be resentful and want to leave. If they know somehow that "I can't live without you!" means "I'll starve without you, you're my daily meal," they won't feel loved and valued for who they are rather than for what service they provide. Vampires have to work hard on openly appreciating their lovers for their own uniqueness, and not let desperation leak through. Tell your lover how wonderful they are, in words and deeds, that show that you appreciate their specific talents and qualities and not just that they are present, loving, and willing to humor you. Buy them the book of their choice and tell them how much you love their intelligence; take them to an event that they love and compliment them on their zest for life. If you think hard enough, you can come up with ways to alleviate their concerns that they're just a walking cafeteria. If you can't come up with anything, then you are not doing them a favor by being with them.

> I actually like being my lover's primary food source. It gives me a great deal of satisfaction to take care of my lovers' needs and this is a wonderfully intimate way to do that. I'm a high-needs lover in my own way, so being needed for this helps quiet my irrational feelings of being more trouble than I'm worth. It is

like having a lover with any other kind of disability. This one needs help getting around. This one needs help lifting things. This one needs a carefully prepared diet. This one needs his money folded and his soup cans labeled. Loving a vampire is no different. There is always the danger in that of feeling more like a nursemaid than a lover, but I think that if you can see that sort of service as an expression of love rather than an annoying chore or an imposition, you can work it out.

–Joshua

When it comes to actual sex, it may take some working out as to who does what when. After you've been drained, you may feel luxuriantly lethargic, or just tired. You may want to be held, or just roll over and go to sleep. Your vampire will probably be hyperactive and energetic, and ready to go twenty more rounds. The aftereffects of a feeding can be like taking a stimulant drug; vampires have described it as "colors are brighter, sounds are louder, sensations are more intense; I want to bounce up to the ceiling". You, on the other hand, may find all this irritating, especially if you just want to get some quiet rest and recoup what you've lost. The feeding pattern may mean that you'll be "down" when your vampire is "up", and when they're unfed it's reversed. On the other hand, some vampires are lethargic and logy after a feeding, while they're "digesting"—and this is especially true for secondary vampires—and they may want to nap or ignore you until they've processed your energy.

Try to work out some sort of accommodation to this. Some partners see to it that the vampire gets fed last, after all other things have been done, so they won't be demanding more sex. In one musician couple, the vampire is trained to hop up after sex and feeding are finished and immediately fix his lover a drink and snack, and then serenade her on the guitar, which gives him something to do with his energy until it "settles", and allows her to relax.

On the other hand, if two secondary vampires are lovers, they have the option of doing a Tantric trick of circulating energy during sex. This exercise is not done to feed one person with the other person's energy; it is a mutual sharing that can encourage bonding and possibly be used for sex magic. It works like this: The partners begin by synchronizing their breathing during the first part of their lovemaking. When enough sexual energy has been raised (which has to be their call), one partner begins to draw energy out of the other partner's body. The other partner then pulls it back out into themselves, and it begins again. Ideally, a circular motion is made, with the energy being pulled out of one partner's upper chakras and then pulled back into the other partner's lower chakras. You can periodically reverse the flow, or the direction.

In the traditional Tantric exercise, lovers push their own energy into each other; the vampire version has them pull it out instead. Some reports of this exercise extol the ecstasy that it adds to sex. It is especially useful as it seems to be easier to convert sexual pushing to a gender-neutral exercise than it is to convert energy pushing during sex, and thus it can be used by any combination of bodies. Some lovers don't even go any further than kissing and body contact; the energy exchange, not intercourse of any kind, becomes the center of the action. Others use it as a tool for intimacy; when a secondary vampire puts their energy through a lover and gets it back again, it is "flavored" with that lover's essence, and can be used to understand them more thoroughly on a deep, spiritual level. Of course, it may not work for some people. Although sexual arousal is one possible response to being "sucked", for some people it is anti- erotic and distracts them from their sexuality. For others, it is erotic, but it pulls energy away from the groin and delays orgasm, which can be used positively or negatively. Your mileage may vary, so try it in small ways first.

As we've mentioned above, being fed on can become a sexual fetish for some donors after a while. Repeatedly synching something up with sex and orgasm can have a profound Pavlovian effect on people, and I've seen folks who went from one vampire to the next in order to get their needs met. Rita, who has had several vampire lovers, wrote to us: "After I broke up with my first vampire—a real jerk and a half who abused me physically—I had trouble with sex for a while. My next few lovers were good people, and good lovers even, but something was missing. After sex, I got up and did my dishes; I wasn't so completely wiped that I could barely roll over and pass out. It took me more than a year to figure out that I'd become accustomed to being fed on, and had associated that state of total lassitude with the way that afterglow was supposed to feel. I only figured it out because I went out with another vampire! Although I'm now monogamous with a man that I love, I'm still drawn to psychic vampires. It doesn't matter if they're the ugliest one in the room; I can smell them, and I'm instinctively drawn to them. When they brush up against my aura, I feel that sucking sensation and I want to melt. Frankly, though, I'd like to get rid of this addiction, because it's not right for me to indulge it now."

Joshua mentions that: "There have been periods where we abstained entirely from feeding—for example, when I was getting Reiki training—and it is frustrating for both of us. He likes to tease that he's gotten me addicted to it, but it is more that the tension created by him holding back his desire to feed creates a tangible barrier between us, no matter how physically intimate we are. After a while I miss him so much that I want to cut myself just to break down that wall."

If you have a primary vampire partner and the two of you decide to have children together, remember that primary vampirism often runs in families. The last couple of months while carrying a primary vampire fetus can be pretty wearing on the mother. (After the baby is born, check Chapter 5: The Family Vampire.) Vampire partners should find another source of prana during the late stages of a pregnant partner's gestation, so as not to place too heavy a load on them. Do this no matter what you think the baby is; pregnancy is hard enough without an external (if loving) parasite. However, if the mother drags around more than usual during the last trimester of her pregnancy, and feels drained, the little one might be to blame. If you can find someone who specializes in Reiki or Ch'i Gong, try to get them regular sessions. If baby breastfeeds, they'll likely feed during that time too, so you might want to continue the sessions after birth for a while.

If it's the vampire who's pregnant, a vampire child can still drain them, and they can need extra energy just to make it through the day. In our experience, the reverse is not true. While the fetus is contained in the mother's aura, her own aura does not differentiate it as a different person, kind of like the way her body doesn't reject it as foreign tissue and expel it. We universally found that primary vampire mothers can't seem to get a fix on the fetus as if it were a separate person, and thus can't feed on it any more than they can feed on themselves. This is probably an evolutionary mechanism, or no female primary vampire could give birth and the genetic anomaly would have died out long ago.

Energy Feeding Ritual for Lovers

Although many vampire-donor partners already have a set routine for feeding, this is a ritual that they can do in order to make it even more special if they choose. It's also good for new lovers who want to try setting up a regular feeding relationship, as it ritually offers consent. The couple may want to prepare for the rite by doing some kind of purification, together or separately. If the vampire half of the couple (or either party, if we're talking about two secondary vampires who switch off) has trouble being close and not feeding, then the purification ritual should be done separately. If the couple is experienced at spending close time together without feeding occurring, then you can do it together.

Suggested things to do as a prelude: Ground and center. Sit facing each other and breathe together, synchronizing your breaths, for a few minutes. Take a long, slow bath together, and wash each other. Light incense and blow it across each other. Dance around each other, without touching, to strong, intense music that you both like. (The dancing can be sexy or just wild; the idea is to rotate around each other like planets without letting your personal space intermingle.) Afterwards, dress in clean, loose clothing, or stay naked.

Have some of your favorite foods prepared, and put small amounts of them on a tray, along with a cup or goblet of water, wine, or fruit juice, depending on your personal tastes. Sit facing each other, on the bed or floor or in chairs if you like. One partner holds up his/her hand, palm facing his/her partner, and the partner places his/her palm against it. For the following lines, #1 is the individual who will be doing the feeding, and #2 is the individual who will be giving out the energy.

1: I am a wanderer in the wilderness, seeking the river of life.

2: The river of life flows within everything. You have found it.

1: The road is long and dusty, and I thirst like the desert sands.

2: Drink of me, for the river is within me.

(The two share the cup of liquid; first the donor holds it to the lips of the vampire and then they reverse the procedure.)

1: I am a child of the Earth, and I seek sustenance from the fire that runs through her.

2: The fire of life runs through everything. You have found it.

1: The night is dark and cold, and I hunger for its warmth.

2: Take sustenance from me, for the fire is within me.

(The two feed each other bites from the tray.)

1: Do you consent to being my fountain of life this night?

2: I consent, but the price is love and trust.

1: I will gladly pay that price.

2: Do you consent to the limits I may set?

1: I consent, but the price is love and trust.

2: I will gladly pay that price.

(Couple kiss, and may continue lovemaking and/or feeding in whatever format they prefer.)

4
The Greatest Gift: Being a Donor

Why would anyone willingly consent to give up their vital energy, their ch'i, to another human being? Well, they might love that human being, or at least like them and care about them, and know that they are in need. Or they might think it feels good, or it might be removing some pain or fear or sorrow. Or it might turn them on. Whatever the reason, being a prana donor doesn't mean that you just get to lay there and be a helpless doormat, no matter what the vampires do in the movies. You are not a victim. You are a consenting adult. Therefore, you have certain obligations, to yourself and your vampire.

If you've consented to be a donor, you have the following responsibilities: First, learn how to say no. If you're not in top shape, be firm and don't give in to your vampire's obvious need. Period. It will set a poor precedent, and they should be working on learning discipline anyway. Second, learn to ground and center, to pull energy up from the earth. You'll need it. Also, learn to shield, to enclose your aura with a firm shell that keeps anything from getting in or out. In the above case of overfeeding, a skilled donor would know to immediately ground and center in order to get new energy flowing in; shield in order to close off the escaping flow, and then carefully visualize closing down each leak. If there's no one around to teach you these things, there are plenty of books on the subject, probably in the same store in which you're buying this one.

You'll also have to learn how to stop them in the middle of the feeding if they get carried away. Vampires who are new at this control thing may not know exactly when to stop, and they need to you tell them when it feels like they're starting to take too much. This means that you, the donor, must also be aware of what's going on. Being fed on will feel different to different people. To some, it always feels like an invasion, and they have to fight to stay open and not shut out a vampire. To others, it may be pleasant, and to still others it may be an incredible sexual turn-on. This is certainly a bonus in terms of reward for the donor, but it may also mean that by the time you get your head together through the clouds of ecstasy, you're going into shock. Start slow. Have your vampire take small amounts, and stop while you still feel like you have plenty left to give. This will help you learn to calibrate your own capacity as well. See the exercises below.

You may also have to deal with another problem. Full-time regular feeders start to get telltale marks in their aura that proclaim to any who can see that they are someone's regular food dish. Who can see it? Why, other vampires, of course. It's unlikely that anyone else will notice, or even know what they're seeing if they do notice, but to other vampires it's like a sign on your forehead. They will be irresistibly drawn to you, which may be a problem. (Most of them probably won't even be aware of why they're attracted.) There are two ways to solve this. One is to do a ritual to have your vampire mark your aura still further, with a kind of "This is my territory; keep off!" astral sign. This is often done by them rubbing you with a drop of their own blood. Since all vampires are instinctively territorial, it'll warn them off. If this isn't your thing, then the other option is just for you to get real assertive, put up good shields, and tell them to get the hell away from you as coldly as you can. Don't get hot and angry or scared; that'll just encourage them.

I discovered this when I got my first full-time donor. We were careful—only did deep feeding through the skin most of the time, occasionally did a little bit of bloodletting for a special occasion—but she did, eventually, develop psychic "ports" in certain areas of her aura where I fed often; sort of semipermanent astral holes formed by our intimacy. She wasn't leaking prana from them; in fact, they formed gradually, and always closed over quickly after each session. However, they seemed to be a big astral label slapped across her aura reading "DONOR", and she drew vampires like flies. Conscious ones, unconscious ones ... they all flocked to her, and began their little games, Since she was a strong woman, she shooed them away, but it became pretty annoying. I suspect that most of them were unconscious, and her vampire-sensitized aura just "smelled" too good to resist.

We discussed the options ... my stopping feeding, for a while or permanently; putting some sort of shield up to hide them; etc. What we finally came up with was a ritual where I "marked" her as my "property"—not physically, only astrally, and only for the purposes of feeding. It was basically the same thing as a predator urinating on the borders of its territory in order to keep out other ones, but it did not bind her or restrict her actions in any way. It worked like a charm, too ... not only did they stop flocking to her, but they often flinched and walked away, strangely uncomfortable.

This kind of ritual, however, should only be taken on by a couple who are real equals, who are both aware of what they are doing and have consented to it, and who have no discomfort with the idea. Wearing someone else's label isn't a comfortable thing for some people, and they shouldn't have to choose between being harassed by other vampires and wearing an invisible ownership tag. The only fair option, if this has become a problem, is to back off and space out the feedings so that the aura can regroup and change. As it ended up, after a year or so she decided that she needed a break from the donor relationship and I psychically "erased" the sign.

The Feeder/Donor's Bill Of Rights:

1. You have the right to say no at any time. It doesn't matter how desperate or sickly your vampire is; if you don't have it to give without endangering yourself at the moment, you have the right to say no. Practice saying no, whenever you can. We know that we sometimes get to feeling desperate, and try to wheedle you into it, but if it doesn't feel right, don't give in.

2. You have the right to demand that your vampire ask you directly for energy, instead of coming around and trying to start an argument, or tease you, or otherwise provoke you into releasing unpleasant energy. You have the right to demand that your vampire be continually working on awareness of their needs, energy levels, and actions, and

that they be honest with you about it rather than driving you nuts with their provoking behavior.

3. You have the right to limit your interaction with any vampire. For some, you may be willing to share your blood, or maybe you don't want to do that at all, ever, with anyone. For others, you may prefer to give only energy. For still others, you may not want to have anything to do with them. This is perfectly acceptable; you are not a public utility. You get to decide what method of feeding will be used, and what level of intimacy and body fluid exchange will occur.

4. If you play with blood sports, you have the right to expect that all instruments used will be sterile, sharp, and safe; to decide the area and set the size and depth limit of any cutting that may be made, and to expect to receive proper antiseptic and aftercare. You have the right to get straight and honest answers from your vampire as to how skilled and/or experienced they are in cutting technique. You have the right to ask for and receive references, and to ask that your vampire demonstrate their cutting ability on themselves or someone else first so you can watch and inspect. You have the right to expect proper aftercare, with daily check-ins for some time if necessary to see how you are doing and if there are any aftereffects. You also have the right to expect to walk away from a blood- offering with all psychic holes adequately patched, as well as all physical ones properly bandaged.

5. If you give away your blood to any vampire in a way that might possibly mix their fluids with yours, you have the right to a full STD testing workup from them, and you have the right to know who else they are doing this admittedly unsafe practice with, and find out how clean those people are. You have the right to demand this testing again if you feel that they have slipped recently and become unsafe. If there is anything going on that makes you feel unsafe, you have the right to say no. (See #1.)

6. You have the right to ask to talk with former, past, or current feeder/donors of any vampire who wants your services. You have the right to be suspicious of any vampire who has no former or past feeder/donors who have anything good to say about said vampire.

This brings us to the question that is probably already in the forefront of your mind...can vampires "convert" people to vampirism, like in the myths? The answer is ... yes and no. You have to be born a primary vampire, and no one can convert you to that. However, anyone can learn to pull energy, as I've said, and I've seen situations where the lover of a vampire becomes so low-energy through continuous feeding that s/he unconsciously starts pulling energy off of other people, becoming a secondary vampire in turn. No one can "convert" you or force you to become one, and sharing blood can only pass on STDs, not vampirism. However, a vampire can teach you, consciously or unconsciously, to do some or all of what they do. You have to learn it yourself, though.

Can a primary vampire make another primary vampire? Yes. I've done it. It has to be done the old-fashioned way, starting from scratch and donating half your chromosomes to the effort. Of course, once you make one, you're responsible for the next 18 years, and then you have to put them through college. Mine was a teenager at the first publication of this book, and I was paying for my "creation-of-another-vampire-sin" by having to listen to her angst-filled catnip-response music all the time.

Exercise D (for donors): *First, learn to ground and center yourself. Sit quietly and visualize yourself like a tree with its roots in the earth, pulling the energy up. Breathe deeply, but don't hyperventilate. Now become aware of your aura, surrounding your body. Feel it, learn how far out it goes from your skin, how dense it is normally (this is especially important), and where it is thicker or thinner. Does it have an edge, like a shield or wall, or does it just fade out? Get to know its healthy manifestation.*

Now let your vampire feed. Go away from them, into another room, and ground and center again. Is your aura changed? How? How does the energy around you in your personal space become different after a feeding? Is it more sluggish, or quicker? If your vampire touched you in a particular place (or drew blood from there) how does it feel, astrally? Hold your fingers an inch away from the space and see what kind of sensations you get. If there's a hole, you'd better patch it up, and complain to your vampire to be gentler. If it's merely a dimple or thin spot (which is usually the case) push energy into it with your hand, and fill it up.

Evaluate your feelings while giving prana. Did it feel erotic, or comfortable, or difficult? If there was discomfort, can you pinpoint where that came from? Did your skin crawl? That's sometimes a reaction to your aura pulling in and tightening up as a defensive response. If there was a feeling of violation, that might be because your aura was trying to fight them, or it might be that you have trust issues and the experience triggers bad memories. For the second problem, we recommend therapy. For the first problem, we recommend getting to know your vampire better and establishing more trust between you, especially physical trust. Ask your vampire to spend time touching you but not feeding; that can help build trust.

Now go do something that normally energizes you—eat, nap, get a Reiki session, take a soothing bath or an invigorating shower, lay in the sun, whatever works. Ground and center and check your aura every couple of hours. How quickly does it return to normal? Compare this to the amount of energy you think your vampire took from you. Then compare it to the amount of energy they actually think they got. (The two amounts may vary, unfortunately. What feels like a lot to one person may be only a piddling amount to another.) Use this part of the exercise to calibrate how quickly your energy regenerates, in comparison to the amount bled off of you.

Exercise E: *Ask your vampire to feed off of you, and then push them away in the middle and walk away. (Warn them first that you are going to do this exercise, please, or there may be fireworks, or waterworks, depending on your vampire's temperament.) If they will go along with it, try doing this* *at different stages. If there is a point at which you can no longer summon the will to push them away, you have two choices. You can do your best to make sure they never drain you to that point by pushing them away before it happens (or asking them to stop), or you can tell them about it and trust them to lay off before you're harmed. The decision rests with you, and how much you trust the competence, honesty, and self-control of your vampire.*

Being a donor is a great act of love. You're helping someone to survive, and be healthier in the world. You're entering honestly, openly, and safely into a relationship that is usually subliminal, deceptive, and dangerous. You're showing both the vampire that you aid, and the rest of the world, that there is an alternative to a society of frantic, predatory leeches and their unwilling victims. You're giving out a mitzvah to the universe, and the universe will reward you. (Actually, the vampire should reward you, too, in some way, or they're not worth it. At the very least they should show up and help you out on moving day.) But you have to keep in mind that you are not the everlasting fountain of life, even if you are a Reiki master or an athlete in superb health.

Remember to put your own health first, or you won't have enough to give out. Take vitamins, eat right, and get lots of rest. If you give blood, know what safe procedure is and stick to it. Take care of all cuts or pricks immediately, and don't let anything get infected later on. If your vampire is your sex partner, be aware of what their sexual practices are. Don't give in to the dream of being sliced by the big decorative dagger, even if it is romantic. The thing is probably crawling with germs. If sex (or anything else) becomes simply a vehicle for feeding your lover, insist of better treatment. Don't let your vampire bully you into anything you don't want, and don't let them behave badly toward you just to get an extra snack. A weak person is no good for a vampire. Strong people not only have more prana, their limits can force us to behave, which sometimes we need, if we're not in full control of ourselves.

And while you're at it, practice saying no. Sometimes saying no can be a great gift as well, as it can show someone something about themselves that they didn't know. There have been people in my life who have said no to me when I was hungry. At the time, I hated them. Now I want to thank them. They showed me the edges of my desperation, and inspired me to do something about it. Without them, I'd still be wandering around alienating people and wondering why.

5
The Family Vampire:
Bringing Up the Next Generation

Primary vampirism does seem to be inherited. My mother is one. My grandmother seems to have been one. My daughter certainly is one; she sucked prana with her mother's milk and showed all the signs from birth. When she was five, I began teaching her about the life force in things. First I explained about auras, and asked her to describe mine; as I had expected, she described the energy pattern around my body pretty accurately. Then I asked her to look at all the living things in the house, and describe their auras, down to the potted plants. Like me, she could "see" or sense them, getting a picture in her mind, without visual cues; I taught her how to navigate her way through the house in the dark by "seeing" where all the potted plants were giving off their muted glow.

By this time, of course, she was long since ensconced in the "provoking" pattern of behavior, which I knew was an instinctive attempt to feed. I started teaching her to monitor her energy levels, and be aware of her hunger. Since, like me, she suffers from mild hypoglycemia (a common vampire ailment), and I had to teach her to monitor her physical blood sugar, it wasn't a far cry to add prana levels to the lesson. When she would storm or fuss or be irrational or cranky, everyone was encouraged first to ask her if she'd eaten food lately, and if she had, if she was "hungry". There wasn't always much we could do about the latter condition, but it helped her see what was unconsciously motivating her.

We also discussed acceptable feeding targets, which for a young child are not too abundant. I was, of course, always willing to feed her, but I was often low energy myself ... and to a primary vampire, another primary vampire's energy often doesn't feel very nourishing. My ex (we were divorced by now) reacted violently, instinctively, whenever she would try to feed deeply. My wife was not willing to be anyone's feeder but mine. It was a difficult time for her.

As she grew older, we were able to make friends with a variety of people who were aware of our family tendencies, and were fine with giving a little bit of prana now and then; they'd let her lay a hand on their arm and "pull" some. Eventually, in her teen years, she started dating and created her own pool. I also taught her how to give back massages while "pulling" aches and pains off, and that made her fairly popular with her circle of friends.

Most child vampires, and nearly all who are young children, will be primary vampires. There are occasional secondary vampires among children, especially if they have had a hard time; one foster parent that I know got a child who was already a secondary vampire at the age of 8 from her rough childhood. However, you can tell the difference by the way they react to energy. Any child would rather have negative attention than no attention, but the small secondary vampire would much rather have positive attention, and may be repelled or frightened by negative emotions. (Things will be a little different for small primaries.) Children who develop secondary vampirism in childhood due to trauma will also come with a host of other problems—low self-esteem, hypervigilance, phobias, etc. as a product of the same unhealthy environment that forced them into vampirism. Pour on the positive attention—they can't get too much of it. At the same time, set the boundary rules as you would for a primary vampire child; they also have to learn consciousness, control, and ethics.

When a primary vampire is born, s/he can often be a sickly child if not given enough attention—the kind that is fussy and unhappy, and calms down only with constant bodily contact. Often s/he will show symptoms of digestive trouble such as colic; this affliction may be outgrown later or bedevil them throughout their lives. I have surmised that this is a matter of dissonance between the astral body and the physical one—while the physical body is nourished by actual food, if there isn't enough prana, the body will still get echoes of a "malnourishment" message which it reacts to with upset physical digestion. As they grow older primary vampires learn instinctively which types of strong energy "taste" best, and by trial and error they learn how to get what they need. By the time we can talk in complete sentences, we have already worked out how to manipulate others into feeding us ... because we have to.

If you have a loving, non-abusive, family where all the children feel loved and safe, and one of your offspring is a primary vampire, they will probably drive you nuts. They will be obnoxious, argumentative, antagonistic, combative, and sometimes manipulative in creating arguments among the rest of your family. (This is not meant to be the only explanation for these traits in a child; children can act like this for a wide variety of reasons including attention deficit disorder, minimal brain damage, stress, anger over a divorce or stepparent or new sibling, brain chemistry problems, bad parenting, or just a particular kind of astrological chart.) The reason for this is that they are instinctively seeking negative energy to eat, and there isn't enough of it around in a reasonably happy family household. Sure, they can get positive energy, but it's the negative stuff that tastes the best. It's the candy that they are willing to go the extra mile to get. This is how you tell the difference between the kid who just craves attention and the primary vampire child: the one would really prefer positive attention but will settle for negative, and the other is strangely drawn to the negative stuff.

In an abusive and dysfunctional family, a primary vampire child is often the best-natured kid around. I grew up in such a family, and I was practically a bloated tick from all the bad stuff swirling through the air. Was I happy? Of course not. I was well fed, and I never did any provoking behavior (at home, anyway), but I was miserable. Just because we are drawn to negative energy, even as children, does not mean that we are not human. We are still hurt by most things that any other child might be hurt by, and we can get just as screwed up living in such a situation as any other kid. If anything, it's even harder for us in many ways; if an adult is angry and/or suffering and/or scared, we simultaneously get negative stimuli (the emotional fear and pain that any child feels when the adults in their lives are in a very bad space) and positive stimuli (being drawn to the center of the storm, and getting fed, and feeling psychically "satisfied"). As you can imagine, it takes some of us decades to work out the results of these conflicting messages on our psyche. Some never work it out completely, and repeatedly end up in strange, abusive relationships later in life.

Similarly, you are not doing your child a favor to unleash your unpleasant emotions on them. Yelling at them will feed them some of your anger, but it will also teach them that angry people are a worthwhile thing to be around, the angrier and more violent the better. The parent of a primary vampire has a very difficult job, and must walk a line between starving their child and traumatizing them.

Later, your vampire child may be drawn to "troublemakers", the kind of kids who are always angry at something and defy authority frequently, creating more anger and pain. All too many times I've seen the "innocent" sidekick, boyfriend/girlfriend, or general best friend and binder of wounds who is actually getting a meal off the "bad" kid. They may subtly or explicitly encourage the risky behavior in order to be sure of getting their next meal.

They may also be the troublemaker themselves. Vampire children with extroverted, assertive personalities may resort to bullying as a way to get their requisite amount of regular negative prana. Even being yelled at by an angry teacher or vice principal—or parent—can be a subtly positive reinforcement. They may also learn the fine art, in their teen years, of needling Mom and Dad into a fury ... figuring out which buttons to push by being unreasoningly argumentative.

Some vampire children have already experienced enough rejection at a young age (often from their clumsy attempts to evoke prana), and developed such a mistrust of people (as well as resenting them for being necessary) that they become loners, often depressed and surly due to prana depletion. Others may be loners by default, if no other children will have them around. Sarah writes: "I was a really unpopular kid, but the girls in my class all wanted me to come to their slumber parties so that I could hypnotize them. I had a natural gift for it. It hurt like hell to be banished to another room after they were tired of using me, and I cried myself to sleep a few times, but it was the closest I got to popularity and I fell for it every time."

Some suggestions for dealing with your vampire child:

1. Try to stay calm when coping with them, as much as possible. Take up meditation and breathing exercises. Count to ten, or a hundred, before getting into a discussion with them. Leave the room and calm down if you're worried about blowing up. This doesn't mean that you're going to go about like Mr. Spock, treating them coldly and unemotionally; it's perfectly all right to shower them with positive affection and happiness. Yeah, it's oatmeal, not filet mignon, but kids can grow up healthily on oatmeal if they have to, and they need to learn that if they have to provoke a response in someone, it's better to try for a positive one.

2. Give them as much physical affection as you can stand, and set good boundaries when you've reached your limit. Vampire children often seem starved for affection—especially physical affection, as it's quite nice to sit inside a larger person's aura and slowly "soak". As infants, they may be calmest when carried around on someone's body, in a sack or backpack, and older kids should know that they can get lots of hugs and cuddles when they need it. When you've had enough, set a firm boundary, and reassure them that they can get more later. They need to understand that they will, eventually, be able to get more energy in this soft, nontraumatizing way; that it will not suddenly vanish, never to return. They also need to understand that being hungry is not an excuse to force yourself physically on another person, even a parent; that everyone has the right to control their own personal space.

This will, of course, get harder when they become adolescents. Most adolescents are not comfortable being affectionate with their parents, and often the parents are no longer comfortable with it either, as there is the implied threat of incestual feelings. In fact, being a teen is often the most touch-starved part of a person's life, as there's no one that it's actually acceptable to cuddle with. Many teens turn to sex with peers out of sheer skin hunger, and an adolescent vampire is especially vulnerable to this. There is also the fact that once they figure out how well fed they are after sex, there's no turning back. This is controversial advice, but it might be better to prepare them heavily with safe sex advice, and help them develop a code of sexual morality that includes honesty and consideration, rather than abstinence, which may well be futile.

3. As soon as they're old enough, explain the situation to them as honestly as possible. If you don't like the word "vampire", make up something else, but please do give them a vocabulary to identify and describe what they're feeling. That way you can call them on it; for example, if your small vampire is behaving particularly badly, you can ask "Are you prana-hungry?" the same way you'd ask an irritable child with low blood sugar if their stomachs need fuel. If they learn to monitor themselves from an early age, they'll have less trouble doing it later in life.

4. Pets are sometimes a good place to get small amounts of prana, especially large benign dogs of the sort that will let toddlers hang on their ears and tails. Cats tend to get up and walk away as soon as you start to feed, except for a few particularly passive and lazy ones. Keep an eye on your child at first in order to make sure that they aren't deliberately annoying the animal. Some people will object to this idea on the grounds that animals can't consent in words, but frankly every cat or dog I've ever had was quite able to consent, if only by walking away if it didn't like what was happening. It's good for children to learn to discern consent from intelligent animals by reading their body language, if only because it will help them later in discerning lack of consent from the sort of insecure human being who says yes and means no, or changes their mind but is too weak to say so. If you have a dog or cat who will sit still for this (and believe me, they know what's going on), make sure that you're there with your child for the first few times, and discuss how they know the animal is OK with it, and when they cease being so.

5. Small psivamps often have difficulty being empathetic to others. It's not that they can't sense other people's emotions, or that those emotions are not real to them—they can, and they are—but you have to keep in mind that they will be drawn to someone who is hurting, and they will eventually get positive reinforcement for someone else's pain. These children need to be shown the consequences of their actions as soon as they can cognitively understand such a thing—shown, not told about or lectured to. How you do this is your decision as a parent, but whenever my daughter had been hurt by someone else, I made comparisons while the wounds were still fresh, as it were. "This must have been how Stephanie felt when you shut her in that box," and so forth. (This actually happened; I found my three-year-old daughter sitting happily on a toybox containing a crying two-year-old friend, feeding contentedly.) We also watched movies, which show people in pain in front of you with no actual source of prana present, and discussed how various characters must have felt, and how that pain resembled something that she had experienced. A psivamp child does not automatically equal a sociopathic adult. Sociopaths don't feel, or care about, the other person's pain; it isn't real to them. Other people's pain is incredibly real to a vampire; it just feels good on a psychic level, although not necessarily on an emotional one. Teach your children to listen to their own feelings on the matter, above and beyond the call of the hunger.

6. Start teaching them the healing powers of their gift at a young age. Even a five-year-old vampire can learn to help take the pain from a friend's skinned and bandaged knee. They need to learn the lesson as young as possible that helping people in need is a Good Thing. When they are older, it might be useful for them to learn massage, or shiatsu or another form of acupressure, as a vehicle for helping people. If they seem drawn to human service work, encourage it, but don't force it. I, for one, can't stand counseling; I'm not nearly good enough at unconditional positive regard.

7. Discourage manipulative behavior. Call them on it at once, and give them an above-board alternative. Try to get it through their heads

that a friend whom you gain power over through manipulation is not a real friend, because they don't love you for who you really are, which is what real friends do.

8. If they feel like they need to be around a bunch of people, let them do it. Often, young psivamps will hang out with large groups of peers (or adults) simply to suck up some extra energy. If they're not naturally extroverted, this can be wearing on them. Be sensitive to their need to go out "hunting", even if only the benign sense of hanging out with other kids, and their need to hole up sometimes and recoup. Understand that if the friends they choose to be with are argumentative, or melodramatic, or angry, they are also tasty. If the peer group is potentially violent, however, you should either step in and help them find a better one, or else teach them the anger-eating exercise and make sure they get good at it.

9. If they have the aptitude for it, encourage them to perform in some way. This can be a matter of presenting things in front of their class, or taking lessons where there is some form of recital, or being children's theatre groups, or stage magic. It's not that psivamps are immune to stage fright, but most of us figure out quickly that the rewards are well worth it. I strongly encourage psivamp kids to run or take part in a haunted house-type event at Halloween, where people willingly lay down money for the chance to be scared and give off all that nice fear vibe.

10. I've met quite a few child psivamps who liked to go to scary movies, less for the movie than for the gleeful fear reactions of the other moviegoers. For that matter, any dramatic theatrical or film presentation which induces strong emotions in the audience—for instance, a rock concert—is a free buffet. Since something like this is basically free emotion-laden prana, floating around for the taking, encourage them to go to such things and feed. Be straightforward and honest about it. If they come home high and buzzing, they'll leave you alone for a few days.

11. Teach sexual ethics to teens. This includes things like not flirting and teasing with someone until they become agonized, merely

to get some sexual frustration out of them, with no actual intention to follow through in any way. It also includes not luring someone into bed simply to get some lunch. Be ready to walk them through their first real breakup; have a tasty (and preferably new and distracting) energy source ready and waiting for the occasion, to help them keep from sliding into obsessive behaviors. Teach safer sex.

> Being a teenager and being a vampire is hard. You don't get much of a good chance to feed. With my boyfriend, I have to catch myself so as not to constantly provoke him. Sometimes I feel like a lamprey, suckering onto him. Once I was with a bunch of adult friends who were out of money and having nic-fits from lack of cigarettes. I told them I'd give them two bucks for a pack of butts if I could take all the prana I wanted from them. They agreed, and their nic-fit frustration actually tasted good. It worked out well for everyone all round.
>
> –Jess, teenage psychic vampire

Exercise F: *To be done with small vampire children, as soon as they are old enough to understand. First blindfold the child (make sure that they are OK with this, and not frightened; make it like a game and keep talking to them as you move about) and place three or four plants in front of them. One should be real; the others artificial silk ones. Have the child hold their hand in front of each plant one at a time, and ask them, "Which one has glowing light around it that you can see with your eyes closed?" It's quite possible that they can pick out the live one.*

If they can't, no harm done; backtrack. Practice looking at things and seeing the aura, or life force, around them. Many if not most vampires tend to see pure prana as a yellow or golden shade; some see it in various different colors. Have your child start with touching living things and describing their aura. When they get to the point where they can see it across the room with their eyes closed, do the blindfold game again, only this time have them navigate through a room blindfolded, using the aura of living plants as markers. Learning this game helped my child be far less afraid of the dark; I placed plants all over in strategic areas so that she could use them for markers on late-night excursions to the bathroom.

*   **Exercise G:** Have your vampire child describe how it feels to feed, what their aura does, how different people "taste". We found it useful to describe people in terms of actual tastes—I reportedly taste like anise; her stepmother tastes metallic, "like the smell of old metal boxes"; a friend tasted "like chocolate pudding". Nausea in sick people was "like melted cheese". Before you can teach them ethics, you have to give them a verbal picture of exactly what it is that they're doing, and it's best if they help fill out that picture. Have them describe the energy of plants, animals (if you have no pets, use a friend's cat and/or dog), and different people. Have them describe whether the energy comes fast or slow.*

6
The Healthy Vampire:
Limits of the Physical

Both kinds of vampires, primary and secondary, can be plagued with physical health issues, although they are often different ones. As was pointed out in former chapters, the well- being of the energetic body affects the well being of the physical body, and vice-versa. This theory is the basis for all kinds of energy healing, from Reiki to ch'i-gong, and it is especially true for psivamps, who often try to prop up the physical health with prana.

One vampire describes herself as having "migraines, which I've suffered from since childhood....my lungs have always been weak ... Theoretically I have myalgic encephalomyelitis (a.k.a. CFIDS). I still test positive for Epstein-Barr virus, but I haven't had a relapse of CFIDS in over a year, so it would appear that I am in remission." However, she has created a regime to keep her going: "I take care of myself. I eat healthy meals, I take long brisk walks, I get enough sleep, and when I start to feel under the weather I go to bed and rest until I'm feeling well again. It's low-tech, but it works for me." Similarly, other autoimmune problems (rheumatoid arthritis, Sjogren's syndrome, lupus, CFS, fibromyalgia, etc) seem to be a fairly common complaint, as are photosensitivity (which might be a secondary symptom of some of these disorders).

As I've mentioned in other chapters, vampires frequently have chronic illnesses. In the case of secondary vampires, some apparently did start (consciously or unconsciously) feeding in order to supplement their illness-drained energy levels. This could be construed as a kind of survival mechanism. With the widespread epidemic of CFIDS and fibromyalgia, which I personally consider to be due to the onslaught of environmental pollution, I've seen more and more unconscious secondary vampires whose feeding behavior began sometime after they were stricken. Strangely enough, this is oddly reminiscent of the rational explanation of the mythical vampire archetype—a wasting disease, usually tuberculosis in those latter days, which seemed to suck the victim dry of his or her life force. The vampiric behavior in those myths tended to start after death, but it is worth wondering if there is a slight half-remembered and misinterpreted connection.

On the other hand, I've met hardy vampires in stunning health who've hardly been sick a day in their lives, so I can't possibly say that illness is the definitive cause of vampirism in all or even most cases. Primary vampires sometimes have chronic congenital illnesses, but again, some are healthy. Even so, there are a few conditions that seem to crop up more often in the vampire population.

One previously-mentioned problem that I've seen vampires suffer from is blood sugar issues. Some are diabetic and some have hypoglycemia. This kind of up-and-down of blood sugar strangely mirrors on a physical level what prana hunger looks like on a spiritual level. This is found in both types of vampires, and I have wondered if it is actually a side-effect of long-term unconscious vampirism, rather than being the other way around. It's possible that having two conflicting sets of hungers can confuse someone, especially as a child or teenager, and create poor eating habits that can permanently affect the blood sugar. It's also possible, since these conditions can be inherited, that in primary vampires they may be genetically linked to whatever genes create the neurological pattern for vampirism.

Another health problem that runs rampant among psychic vampires is that of eating disorders. In nearly every case, the eating disorder was linked to an inability to tell the physical needs from the astral needs—in other words, what sort of hunger was this, and where was it coming from? The most common eating disorder among vampires is, ironically, overeating food when hungry for prana. There's a romantic notion that vampires tend to be thin, but this is no more the case than it is in the rest of our society; there are plenty of overweight vampires who got that way because they unconsciously tried to assuage a prana-hunger by feeding the stomach. Since one does get a bit of a pleasant chemical sensation from eating, especially foods high in sugar and chocolate, it may provide enough of a boost to temporarily convince the vampire that it's working, and they'll do it again, and again.

To be fair, this is not the only cause of overweight; there are a variety of endocrinological and hormonal causes as well, and it should not be foolishly assumed at any time that all fat people are frustrated vampires. Indeed, one of the major causes of slow metabolism is erratic eating habits—the body decides that this must be a famine, and slows everything down. Vampires often tend to have sluggish metabolisms, possibly due to the body's fluctuating prana levels, possibly due to eating erratically rather than in steady meals, most likely a combination of the two.

If underfed vampires tend to develop eating disorders of overeating, vampires who get fed regularly tend to develop the opposite problem, or undereating. Sometimes a vampire can work so hard taking care of their prana supply that they forget about the physical body. Sometimes they even have the idea that as long as they are well-fed pranically they don't need real food. Unfortunately, to burst the bubble of these types, you cannot replace protein and calories with prana. It doesn't work. It's like saying that getting regular oil changes in your car will eventually obviate the need for gasoline. It may increase your mileage, but sooner or later you are going to have to pony up at the pump.

Part of the problem is that there are a lot of psychic vampires out there who really resent being in a physical body. They'd secretly rather be "breatharians" if they could, and when they get properly fed it is such a revelation in feeling that they ecstatically figure this will hold them forever. An example of this is a young vampire I know who was the only psivamp among her siblings in a family with a psivamp father and a nonpsivamp mother. Her father often took her aside and taught her things about how to manage her talent; one day he gave her a freshly picked apple and told her to hold it, smell it, and draw the prana out of it. She found this so mesmerizing that she quit eating, only pulling prana out of fruits and vegetables over the next few days. It was discovered when she passed out from low blood sugar, and her father scolded her and made her promise to eat food regularly.

It's important to eat enough protein and calories to keep your body in tune, or the malnourishment will create a drag on the system that will raise the prana-hunger, yet taking in extra prana will not solve the problem. The best plan is to get very good at recognizing the difference between prana-hunger and body-hunger, and give the needs of both equal time and respect; to "treat them both as two guests in your house", to paraphrase Kahlil Gibran. If you know that you tend to erratic eating, take regular vitamins and supplements, and eat high-protein food when you do eat.

Secondary vampires should keep in mind that doing anything psychic does burn calories. Energy workers have often found this out the hard way; one sits on one's butt doing something magical, or doing Tarot readings, or whatever, and afterwards you feel like you ran a marathon and could eat a whole pig. While feeding for a primary vampire seems to be a no-calorie proposition, secondary vampires may well find that the actual act of feeding will use up physical, bodily energy, and you might need to feed your body afterwards.

Prana-feeding does alter the senses; at least temporarily for a period of several minutes after feeding, many of us have noticed that colors are brighter, sounds are louder, and scents are stronger. It's a short altered state, in which everything is cranked up, rather like the experience of methamphetamine. For some vampires, that fades quickly; for others, it can cause permanent heightening of the senses. Eating food can become an overwhelming sensory issue of chewing and swallowing and texture and taste, much like what occurs with attention deficit disorder, where the input can no longer be screened out. In this case, eating food can seem disgusting.

However, we also come with generally strong wills, and mental exercises can be done to shield the senses so that ordinary eating can occur. The inability to screen out sensory input at will is not an indicator of enlightenment, especially when it interferes with one's physical survival. Try to find food that isn't disgusting to you, but if that leaves you with a nutritionally inadequate diet, that's a loss of control on your part, and you need to work on it. Remember, starving the body affects the energy meridians, just as starving the energy meridians affects the body. You are a package deal. Short of suicide, you have to learn to live here in this flesh.

Migraines also seem to run rampant through the vampire community. Since I've had one sort of dull headache, when I've been in a low-prana state, and another sort of very hard, sharp headache from "overdosing", I suspect that they may be an effect of abrupt energy changes as well. Sarah Dorrance suggests that: "during the attack you should try to put yourself in a trance. I know this is asking a lot, I often have a hard time doing it myself, but it's a good pain control technique. Count backwards and forwards from 500 until you have mesmerized yourself into a state of light hypnosis. Other methods of pain management include analyzing the pain (observe it as if from outside and describe it in detail—this often detaches you from yourself) and biofeedback ... Good preventive medicine in this case is, of course, to make sure you feed regularly. If you are a sangunarian, get blood. If you can't get blood, eat stuff that is high in pranic energy/life force: live culture yoghurt, live bean sprouts, raw tubers and vegetables, dairy products, etc. If you don't really do the blood thing, but prefer to get your life force in another manner, try to do so regularly and remember to ground and centre afterwards."

Remember that any fresh vegetable that can still draw water up through its stem or roots is still very much alive. It's something that most vegetarians don't like to think about; the fresher the food, the more likely it is that you are chowing it down while still awake and kicking, at least on an energy level. Studies done with plants have shown them to be a lot more conscious than we give them credit for. I'm not saying that we shouldn't eat raw food; in may places in the world, they eat raw bugs and eels. We humans—and especially we vampires—are omnivorous predators, and that's the way of it. But if you are a vampire looking for that extra tiny bit of prana, the fresher the vegetables, the more likely they are to "scream" as you eat them, so to speak. It's all the more reason to have a garden, if you have the space.

As Sarah points out, fresh organic yogurt has live cultures that can be eaten and absorbed. Raw yeast also has life in it, but the yeasty-beasties are all killed off by baking yeast in bread. You can get raw brewer's yeast at the health food store; many people swear that it gives hair more sheen and luster. Raw dairy, straight out of the cow or goat or sheep, is nearly as good as blood in many ways. Like blood, it will lose its prana if it's allowed to sit around. Pasteurization also kills it fairly immediately. Although it's illegal nearly everywhere in this country to sell raw dairy, there is much bartering for it among the neighbors of small dairy farms. Make sure that the animals are all inspected daily, and preferably hand-milked. Unpasteurized milk is safe as long as the animals are healthy, and in fact it's technically easier to digest. Milk comes with all the enzymes needed to digest it; we just burn those off as part of the pasteurization process. Organic milk is best, as the animal will not be laden with antibiotics and hormones. Drink it there, fresh and warm from the animal; if warm milk doesn't suit you, you can mix in chocolate or some other flavor that lends itself well to warmth.

Another common vampire ailment seems to be chronic allergies, often to a wide variety of substances. I'm a primary vampire, and I was practically born with allergies to a number of petroleum-based substances such as pesticides and chemical fertilizers, and many artificial chemicals and additives. Vampires with chronic allergies also tend to develop asthma in response, which may further curtail their ability to exercise properly. Again, it's possible that the roller-coaster effect of energy ups and downs in a chronically unfed vampire can oversensitize the body, making it lash out inappropriately at the wrong targets. I've also run across a sizeable number of vampires who had family histories of immune problems; either overactive or underactive, and sometimes both by turns.

When someone suffers from low prana for a lengthy period of time, the first physical response of the body is a lowered immune system. This makes the individual prone to colds, flus, and other bugs that come by, lowering their immunities still further and putting more stress on the low-energy body. This can become a vicious circle, grinding someone into a state of chronic ill health from which it is very hard to recover. It can happen both to vampires, and to the donors that they feed on (especially the unwilling, unaware donors of unconscious vampires). Both sides of the equation should work on their health as much as possible; periods of time spent apart (with lots of good food, rest, vitamins, immune-boosting herbs, and moderate exercise) might help for a drained donor to recoup enough of their energy to keep going. This may be hard on the vampire, but an ethical vampire ought to care deeply about the health of their food source, and not just because they want to keep the tap running.

Sarah again: "Vampires are prone to stress and fatigue disorders because we are like black holes—sucking in massive amounts of energy, then blowing it back out. We're the original 'gas guzzlers'—fuel-inefficient in the extreme. We burn out easily. Being told that we're nuts because we think we are vampires doesn't help matters any. Donors are prone to fatigue as well, if they are drained too much or at inopportune times. Donors can also suffer from stress due to empathic links with their vampire contacts ... We vampires (and our donors) should all be practicing basic stress management. Perform yoga or meditation; exercise regularly to work off steam; watch cartoons; whatever. Eat right. Don't live on a diet of caffeine if you are one of the lucky people who can have caffeine without getting migraines. Sleep is also important—get at least six hours of sleep a night if you can."

Some psychic vampires do report using their talents to keep them alive in the face of life-threatening conditions. Michelle, a psychic vampire interviewed for this book, was born with a ventricular septal defect—in layman's terms, a hole in her heart. Although it was surgically partially closed with a piece of Teflon at the age of four, she still suffers from "a severe heart murmur and occasional bouts of arrhythmia. Additionally, I have a very low heart rate, and my hands are almost always remarkably cold. If I feed on a regular basis, I suffer no ill effects from these conditions, and the arrhythmia is infrequent if not altogether gone. However, when I am unable to feed, the first thing to be affected is the rhythm of my heart."

Some of the vampires who utilize this talent as a survival skill have stories of near-miraculous recoveries from life-threatening illnesses as children, only to later realize that they had been, and were, supporting their lives with other people's juice. As an example, Michelle writes, "I 'fasted' for about eight months once in an attempt to determine if there was any way I could wean myself from taking the life-energy of others. This rather masochistic experiment culminated with my collapse in English class one afternoon at college. I was hospitalized, and the arrhythmia and other difficulties I was experiencing were enough to inspire the doctors to suggest that I go on a waiting list for a heart transplant. Unhappy with the prognosis, I left the hospital and fed that night from my partner. The next day, all symptoms were gone and I was able to swim and work out for 45 minutes at the college rec-center … That experience was a real defining moment in my acceptance of my vampirism; I knew that there was no turning back. It was a little defeat for me, really, to acknowledge that I could not walk away from it; that this was something I had to do, now and for the rest of my life, like a diabetic must eventually come to terms with the constant necessity of insulin shots."

Ron, a secondary vampire from California, writes: "I contracted HIV from unsafe sex over a decade ago. My lover broke up with me, and my energy plummeted. I was afraid to make any new relationships for years, because who'd want someone with AIDS? And that's what I had, within a year; the disease moved very fast as soon as I couldn't keep getting the energy supply that I'd become accustomed to. Fortunately, I prayed a lot, and the Powers That Be sent me a new lover, who understands and lets me feed when I need to. We don't share blood, as that would endanger him, but since I've been feeding regularly my T-cell count is astonishingly better and my symptoms are temporarily mostly in remission. I do believe that without my lover I would be dead in a year, which puts a weird twist in our relationship.

It's strange to actually be dependent on someone for your very life. It would probably be disastrous if he wasn't such a wonderful person. He's pointed out that he's young, strong, and healthy, he loves me, and he knows that he's going to outlive me by a long stretch; he says that he's willing to do what it takes to keep me alive until it's time for me to go, and get every minute out of our life together that he can."

Exercise H (for health): *Write down all the things you do to keep your body healthy. If you're not doing anything, please change your habits. You don't need to be an ultrajock, but the better off your body is, the less prana you'll need to keep up to standard. If you have a chronic illness, at least work on a healthier diet and as much gentle exercise as you can stand, even if only spaced in small amounts throughout the day. Take more vitamins and minerals. Adapt your routine so that when you feel tired and logy, you replenish your body first, wait a while, and then only resort to hunting for prana if you're sure it's not working.*

Exercise I (for insides): *Sit quietly, ground and center, and let your consciousness flow through your body, area by area. Are there places you can't seem to "see" or touch with your internal senses? Are there areas that seem thinner, or weaker, or need to be cleaned up? Go see someone who is more skilled than you at reading health though auras and ask them to check you over. (Don't feed while they're doing it, as it can distract them and screw up the reading.) See if they can find trouble spots that can be worked on. For example, thyroid problems will make anyone feel tired and weak; if they see a problem in your throat area, you might consider having it medically checked out.*

7
The Blood Is The Life

This chapter brings us to that pariah of practices, blood drinking. Fresh blood contains a great deal of prana that fades slowly after leaving the body, but not everyone has the "live energy" receptors to utilize it. Both types of vampires can pull energy from blood, although primary vampires are more efficient about it (as it comes naturally to them rather than being a learned art) and can get a lot more energy from a lot less blood.

Some people will be horrified, or at least uncomfortable, that I have even included a chapter on blood sports in this book. I am certainly not implying that all psychic vampires do or should ingest human blood, but a sizeable portion of them do. There is an entire subculture of "sanguinarians", as they prefer to be called, and many came to that subculture only after making a lot of dangerous mistakes. There are probably vampires out there right now, as we speak, who are starting to experiment with blood play, and they may or may not know how to do it safely. About one in four of the psychic vampires that I know have experimented with it; if you count only the vampires who take part in the S/M/fetish subculture, I'd make it 100%.

(As a disclaimer, I must point out that not all sanguinarians are psychic vampires. Although there is some overlap, there are people who ingest the blood of willing humans for many other reasons: as a sexual fetish, as a form of intimacy, for religious/spiritual purposes, as a form of recreation, etc. This book is not the place to discuss the many and varied permutations of this particular section of the population; that's someone else's job. Suffice it to say that this chapter is for psychic vampires who are also sanguinarians at times, those who straddle the border of both communities.)

To leave out a thorough explanation of safe blood play in the hopes that no one is actually trying it is as stupid an assumption as the idea that telling teenagers not to have sex will prevent them from doing it. In both cases, many of them will do it anyway, and probably not safely. We must remember that Silence Equals Death, and that more harm is done from too little education and too much ignorance than from the opposite situation. If you don't have anything to do with blood play, and never will, and would never date anyone who did, feel free to skip this chapter. If you do (or intend to do) blood-feeding with other people, we have created this chapter with safety advice from professional piercers, cutters, and other body modification people, folks who deal with other people's blood in a non-medical setting on a regular basis.

However, to be on the safe side legally, here's my disclaimer: I am not actually advocating here that anyone take up the ingestion of human blood. It can be extremely dangerous and even deadly if great care is not used (and sometimes, even if it is). Do so at your own risk, and don't say I didn't warn you. However, if you must—or if you already are—here are the safest guidelines we could come up with.

The Centers for Disease Control and the various safe sex organizations have, as far as we could tell after much research, absolutely no guidelines about drinking human blood. This has less to do with its safety or unsafety and more to do with the fact that they are basically horrified by the idea that anyone would be doing it at all, and refuse to countenance such a concept. Our correspondence with them basically resulted in replies of "Ewww—why would anyone do anything like that? And no, we don't have any data on it." Because of this lack of information, we are forced to assume the worst.

The clear and present danger in blood drinking is that in this day and age of many blood-borne diseases, it's just plain unsafe to do promiscuously. (I'm not just talking about HIV, either; there's herpes, and hepatitis A, B, and C, and syphilis, some strains of which are now antibiotic-resistant.) No matter how attractive you find it, you need to do it the same way you would unsafe sex—find a partner with whom you agree to be bodily fluid monogamous (this means that the two of you agree to have any unsafe sexual activities only with each other), get tested for damn near everything, wait six months, and then don't ever "accidentally" slip up with someone else. Period. I cannot recommend any other method for safety. In any other situation, you are taking certain risks. If you are willing to take them, that's your decision, and you can bear the potential consequences yourself.

Drinking someone's blood is at about the same risk factor as sharing dirty needles. While stomach acid is pretty good at destroying things, the problem is that the mouth is often full of tiny cuts or lesions; if you have gingivitis, or if your gums have ever bled while brushing your teeth, you need to understand that this will facilitate blood-to-blood contact. In the end, just as many people will engage in unprotected sex, many sanguinarians will engage in blood-drinking with people who are not fluid bonded with them. This is an individual choice, but remember that it is much better to be safe than sorry. All the prana anyone can give you won't cure you of a fatal disease.

(Also, while you're disqualifying people, remember that there are various small illnesses that you can catch from sharing bodily fluids that aren't fatal, but could be a bummer if you get a germ or virus for a week. Make a thorough—and I do mean seriously intrusive—search into the health of your donor. If they won't be forthcoming, you don't want to play. Oh, and while you're at it, remember that you need to inquire about any drugs, legal or otherwise, or medications that they may be taking. You will ingest some; whether it will be enough to matter will depend on the medication. I can get a mild allergic reaction if I deeply kiss someone who has just ingested penicillin. If the person has been drinking, cutting can be more dangerous; not only will you get some of it, but alcohol thins the blood and inhibits clotting, so it's dangerous for them.)

There is some rumored information in the idea that blood, once removed from the body and placed in a container—like a wineglass, for instance—and ingested after several minutes, will be free of HIV because that virus cannot survive outside the body for more than about seven seconds. However, that seven-second time limit is referring to dried blood, not a glassful of congealing liquid, so don't bet your life on it. Besides, other viruses last a lot longer; hepatitis C can live in even dried blood smears for days, and it's just as fatal in the end. There's also the fact that blood loses prana fast once it gets out of the human aura; even if it were safe at that point (a fact of which we cannot be sure) it wouldn't be good for much from a psychic vampire's point of view.

The other danger about this practice is that you can really hurt someone if you're not skilled and not careful. If you're with an experienced donor, let them do the job. It'll be safer, as they'll know what sort of cut or prick is best for them. Of course, some donors can't bring themselves to cut or prick their own skin, or want it done in an area that they can't reach properly. In that case, you'll have to do the job, and you'd better be careful. Remember that a nasty, painful experience for a first-time donor will probably make them want to run away and never do anything like this again. For an experienced donor, a bad episode may at least make them want to run away from you. Be sensitive to their needs. Read the emotional and spiritual safety precautions below, as well as the physical ones.

Here are the safety procedures for blood-drinking:

1. The safest way to do it is a prick with a diabetic lancet. These can be found in any drugstore, and you can even get the kinds that come in a springloaded device that will prick the skin with the push of a button. If you absolutely want to use a medical syringe to withdraw from a vein, please take a class in phlebotomy so that you'll know what you're doing, or search the BDSM scene for people who give classes in such things. However, it's neither necessary nor entirely safe to go fishing around in someone's veins and removing whole vials of blood. It's better to use medical "stickers" or a very sharp sewing needle (leather needles are good). Any blades or needles that have not just come out of a sterile package should be boiled for 10 minutes, and/or soaked in a 1:10 water/bleach solution. (There are also products on the market for liquid cold sterilization; ask your pharmacist.) Do Not use your teeth to break skin. This is not Hollywood and your teeth are jagged and germ-caked. Don't think that doing it with a pair of sharpened theatrical fangs will work well either.

2. Most vampires prefer to use some sort of blade, because there's more control. Keep in mind that anything used to cut the skin should be cleaned thoroughly, and then the wound cleaned again with antiseptic afterwards. Remember, you're trying to be good to your donor. They are your fountain of life force. Don't mess them up. That big dramatic bowie knife is probably far less safe than a little razor blade. (Don't use X-acto knives, as they come coated with an oil that is not conducive to healing.) Also, the sharper the blade is, the better. I use a tiny Damascus-steel shaving razor, which is so sharp that cuts can't actually be felt. After using, clean your blade thoroughly with water, soap, antiseptic, and bleach; wipe completely dry so as to prevent rust, and keep it in a clean sealed plastic bag, not under your pillow. The plastic bag will keep it clean, but it still has to be sterilized just before each use. (If your blade develops any rust, you can't use it for cutting ever again. Even scouring off the rust may leave tiny particles.)

The best blade, for safety issues, is a prepackaged sterile disposable one-use scalpel blade that you throw away afterwards. These can be obtained mail-order or online through veterinary supply companies. Unlike needles, the numbered sizes refer to shape and not size. The best shape to use is a #10. However, scalpels require a lot of practice. When you first use one, you should apply no pressure at all; just lightly trace the blade across the skin. Applying pressure will have the blade slicing down into muscle. It may take a few seconds before blood will start to show up in the lines; rubbing or smacking the area before cutting will bring more blood to the surface. But don't be impatient and cut further just because you don't see blood in the first second. Waste a few scalpels practicing on tomatoes before you ever apply them to human beings. If you're used to duller knives, don't do something stupid like test the edge with your finger when you pull it out.

3. You should sit quietly for a moment and calm yourself before doing any sort of cutting or pricking. Heat-of-the-moment cutting can be messy, and shaky, nervous hands can make jagged marks or cut far too deep. Your headspace should be calm, serene, and centered. You should be focusing on both the task and the emotional condition of

your donor, and nothing else. Don't get distracted by greed, lust, or blood hunger. Lock all mobile pets out of the room, as they can jump on you at inopportune moments, or smell the blood and want some. Turn the phone ringer off, so that it won't ring and distract you at a critical moment. (You should already have scheduled plenty of quiet time with no interruptions; it ought to go without saying that this is not a "quickie" sort of practice.)

4. Big flashy cuts are Not Good. You can get all you need from one to three little cat-scratch paper-cut-size wounds that will heal up easily. (By little I mean half an inch or so ... and that's length, not depth; depth should be as shallow as you can manage and still get any blood to well up.) There's also no need to take a lot. Blood fresh from the body is so prana-packed that a few drops will keep any vampire surviving for days. Although it may look romantic rolling in a scarlet flood over the skin, the truth is that if you can't get it all easily with your mouth, and have the flow completely stemmed by the time you come up for air, you cut too much and are endangering your donor. Again, I recommend practicing on the skin of a tomato; you should be able to make marks in it without the skin peeling apart. You only want to cut the top layer of the skin, not all the way through it. Cutting in an X will get more blood out of a smaller cut, but also leave more of a scar.

5. Safe places to make shallow cuts are: Chest (not near armpits). Upper back (not near the spine). Outside of upper arms, well above elbows. Outside of the thighs, well above knees. Buttocks (although this can discomfit someone later, when they need to sit for any period of time). Do not cut near joints, underarm, inner thighs, hands, feet, head, and face. Do not cut the neck. Yes, it's romantic, but the skin is way too thin and there are way too many blood vessels close to the surface. You can cut on the top of the shoulder in back,

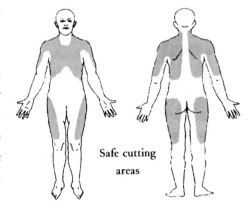

Safe cutting areas

the meaty part of the upper trapezius where it joins the neck; this can "read" like the neck for those who want that intimacy. Safe places to prick with a needle or sticker: All of the above plus forearms and the padded parts of a fingertip. Remember, don't waste. It's safest to avoid all veins and arteries by several inches. That way you won't have to worry about serious accidents.

6. Before you break the skin, wash it with soap and water, and then put something antiseptic on it. If you are going to be using your mouth on the cut, you don't want that to be something that will make you sick. I use a herbal tincture of rosemary and myrrh (both antiseptic herbs) in very high-proof alcohol. One or two drops will do the trick, and it won't poison me like methyl alcohol or Betadine. (However, alcohol will not kill all blood-borne diseases; some, such as hepatitis, cannot be killed with anything that is actually safe to ingest, so there is a certain amount of risk here.) To be fair, the mouth is also a dirty place. There are lots of germs growing in it, and they can get into the wound.

If you really want to be safe, you can rinse your mouth thoroughly with antiseptic mouthwash no more than 5 minutes before you suck on any broken skin. (This is the protocol for healing tongue piercings.) This will reduce the amount of bacteria in your mouth that might grt into the wound. Of course, this may leave a flavor that may interfere with tasting the blood, so you'll have to decide how important that is to you. Don't brush first, as that can create bleeding gums. Afterwards, when you're all done, put on more antiseptic (this time something stronger than alcohol) before bandaging the wound. Make sure you check with your donor to find out if they're allergic to any antiseptics.

7. Aftercare is especially important. Clean, bandage and cover the cutting, no matter how much you or they want to admire it. Stay with them and make sure that they are all right. Donors may be physically hungry after a bloodletting. If they are cold or shaking, they're going into psychic shock. Since we will assume that you only took a few drops of blood, this means that you screwed up and took too much prana. See the emergency directions in chapter 2.

It's possible for someone to go into physical shock just from the pain, which has happened often in piercing or tattoo shops. Even a little ear piercing has made some people pass out, so if your donor does seem to be in distress, try to ascertain what's wrong. Holding them may help, and couldn't hurt. A cool cloth on the forehead may bring them back to their body, assuming that you've not shed enough of their blood to be a physical problem. If the blood won't stop flowing and you realize that you've screwed up and cut too deep, use first-aid techniques to stanch the blood and get them to a hospital immediately. What, you don't know what those techniques are? Find out! This is easily learned in a Red Cross basic first aid class, something that I recommend for anyone who is planning to break human skin.

8. Both you and your donor should be honest about the fact that this practice may leave scars, even if only small, delicate ones. Not everyone wants scars. You can help things with Vitamin E oil and aloe vera, but if you do this frequently, you will get a certain amount of scarring sooner or later. Cuts should be placed so as not to show. Some people heal easily and quickly, and some make awful keloids; hopefully your donor knows which they are. Keep in mind that when most people see someone with a lot of small scars, they may assume that the person is a traumatized self-cutter, which may or may not make your donor uncomfortable. Be considerate and negotiate the placement and shape of each cut, and if they say that they've had enough, it's enough. Vitamin E oil applied to the wound as soon as it closes will help reduce scarring.

9. You can't make your donor keeps their wounds clean. Some people are better at it than others. If they always seem to get infected, they may be less than meticulous about their hygienic practices, or else their immune system may be weak. (Yes, there can be lots of reasons besides AIDS that this could be the case, including several genetic disorders.) Either way, you should stop using them as a donor. Although checking on them is taking responsibility for your actions, they are adults (one would hope!) and you are not their mother; you shouldn't have to oversee them every minute.

10. Don't drink a lot of blood. First of all, you shouldn't be taking that much anyway. Second, blood is very rich and tends to curdle in the stomach. If you drink more than, say, an ounce, you may well get sick and throw up, which isn't going to make your donor very happy, or you for that matter. Human blood passes through the body undigested. No, you won't get nutrients from it like you would animal blood. Your body is designed like that, so that you won't digest yourself in the case of a peritoneal leak. The blood may show up in your fecal material later as a dark color, so be warned.

11. Some sanguinarians like to ingest menstrual blood, as it's going to be wasted anyway, and does not harm the donor to take it. They advise that the best time to ingest it is about three days into the woman's cycle, when the initial blood clots have passed and the final clots have yet to come out. Others find that it tastes "dead", and has little more prana than, say, saliva or sweat. It is true that animals react differently to the smell of menstrual blood than to fresh blood from a wound; there is clearly some chemical difference there. Your mileage may vary.

12. Both vampire and donor should be aware of all the safety procedures being used. Having both parties read this list is a good idea. Some of the procedures still have a certain amount of risk, and everyone involved should be aware of this, and have knowingly consented. Discuss beforehand what will and will not be done. Informed consent is the litmus test of ethical behavior.

My biggest ethical code is 'waste nothing'. Waste bothers me. I see a lot of it in society, and it makes me angry. So I always recycle, I carry an organ donor card, I never make or order more food than I can eat, unless I plan to eat leftovers ... and I never make such a large cut that a single drop of blood is wasted. I make a shallow cut with a sterile, unused razor blade on the back or chest. That way it avoids veins, arteries, major organs, tendons, etc. It's enough to draw a trickle of blood immediately to the surface, but not enough to require direct pressure or come near any muscle. I try to avoid fatty areas because fatty tissue doesn't have much blood in it. Sometimes I make two parallel lines, sometimes I make a crossmark. I clean the wound afterward with antibiotic ointment and Vitamin E oil to minimize scarring, and cover it with a bandage.

                                                            –Sarah Dorrance

Some folks recommend that you practice on yourself first. This is a good idea, but with one caveat: Vampires who get a taste for blood drinking start to find any blood tasty-looking, including their own. If you cut yourself, see your own blood, and succumb to a sudden urge to drink it, you wouldn't be the first vampire who ended up self-cannibalizing. This can be extremely destructive, even suicidal; at the least you'd get no prana from it and you'd weaken yourself still further; at the worst you'll start looking at the veins on the inside of your wrists someday and have a strong urge to open them up. If you find yourself going down that path, cease all blood-drinking immediately until you're quite sure that you won't go there again. If you fear it as being a possibility, don't even try it. Stick with deepfeeding through the skin.

I'm actually quite curious to find out if a certain percentage of traumatized self-cutters are actually psychic vampires who got into this damaging hobby and couldn't stop. Minor-age vampires who start playing with self-cutting are at risk for being institutionalized, as it is unlikely that any shrink will understand something like vampirism and blood-hunger. It's not worth it to lose your freedom, especially when you are merely weakening yourself further. There's also the fact that I'm strongly in favor of having two people in the room whenever a cutting is done, so that there's someone to go for help in case something goes wrong. Doing cuttings alone is just too dangerous, for a variety of reasons.

In fact, if you're worried about becoming too dependent on this practice, you should think again about it. This is only for people with really strong wills who can go without it for long periods of time. After all, if you expect to live a normal life span, there will be times when you simply won't be able to get blood, possibly for years at a stretch, and you should be able to cope without it. Be realistic. Work on finding ways to cope, or don't even get started with it.

Many sanguinarian vampires incorporate blood-drinking into their lovemaking practices; after all, if you're going to be restricting yourself to one person, probably a lover, why not? Sarah points out that: "How much more intimate can one get, emotionally, than to say, 'I trust you with my very life'? My partner trusts me not to get psychotic with the razor. I trust my partner to be free of disease. Either way, it's all about absolute trust."

If you're able to draw prana off of animal blood, make sure that you go about getting it in a manner that is both ethical and safe. First, the safety part: Factory farming is often unclean, and can produce such lovely substances as salmonella, botulism, and E.Coli in uncooked meat products. Drinking raw blood from such places is taking your life into your own hands. There's not much prana in meat that's been dead for more than a few minutes anyway. You can get a hunting license and hunt your own, but that takes skill and is restricted to certain seasons of the year. If you have the space and the temperament, you can keep your own livestock—even backyard rabbits—but that's a lot of work and only for those who enjoy it.

An even better bet is to make friends with small farmers and homesteaders who keep and butcher their own livestock, and offer to help. As a small farmer myself, I can tell you that butchering animals, especially large ones, is a lot of work and an all-day project. Farmers are often glad of an extra pair of hands to turn the meat grinder, help with the skinning, run trays of meat to the kitchen, etc. They vary in open-mindedness, of course, but many wouldn't mind if you hold a pan under the critter's severed neck when it bleeds out, and count that as your pay. You don't have to use the V-word; you can just tell them that you like to eat fresh raw blood for health reasons and you don't trust the abattoir's sanitation measures. Of course, you have the right to inspect the farmer's setup and make your own decisions as to his/her animals' health.

If you do keep and/or kill your own, please adhere to the Pagan code of ethical butchery. This states first that:

A) Animals must be kept in conditions of adequate space, adequate food, adequate hygiene, food that is appropriate to their species, and kind, gentle treatment. It doesn't matter if you're going to kill them in three days; make their last days comfortable and content.

B) Always kill an animal quickly and cleanly. The best way to kill a four-legged critter is a bullet to the head. No animal should suffer as part of its death. We strongly recommend against hanging them upside down and cutting the throat while still alive; this is painful, cruel, and fills the blood (and meat) with unwanted and unhealthy adrenalins. If you aren't skilled enough to kill cleanly, find someone else who is.

C) Butchering should be done in an atmosphere of respect and reverence, not disgust or black humor or sadism. This is for your spiritual benefit as well as that of the animal. Make an offering of something to the spirit of its species—Bull Spirit, or Goat Spirit, or Rabbit Deva—if only of a prayer, or special food, or incense.

Blood is a sacred substance. The biblical phrase that titles this chapter is an oft-quoted one in vampire communities, but many toss it off without really thinking about it. Blood is not just a carrier of the red blood cells that bring you oxygen, the white blood cells that fight disease, and the water that keeps you hydrated; it is also full of your life force. In ancient times, it was believed that every human being was originally made of menstrual blood that clotted in the womb to form a fetus. The Mother Goddess herself was said to have created the world this way, from her own sacred blood. All rivers were the blood of the Goddess, but iron-rich ones represented particularly her sacred menstrual blood. Chalice Well in Glastonbury, former holy site of the goddess Brigid, has "red water", meaning it is iron-rich and tinted red like blood. It runs into a second stream with chalky "white water", which symbolizes semen, and the two mingled together embody the male and female joining in a sacred marriage.

Blood was also a symbol of kinship throughout most of history, which showed in the practice of making "blood brothers" and "blood sisters" by two people exchanging blood through cuttings. Since genetic information was though to be stored in the blood, sharing blood helped to blend one's "bloodlines". Such mingled cuttings are practiced at certain weddings to this day, symbolizing two partners joining as if they are kin.

However, the reverence for blood eventually turned to fear. Many of our ancestors also created customs to keep people away from menstruating women and people with open wounds, claiming that the touch of blood would weaken people, sour milk and dry up cows. Bleeding women were exiled to moon huts to wait out their time. Today, when the taboo against blood has become almost hysterically fearful, its power is stronger than ever. People who were not originally afraid of the sight of blood now flee it in terror. Every time you come in contact with an unknown person's sacred red stuff, you run the risk of eventual death. It's almost as if centuries of wrongly believing that blood could harm angered some deep power so much that S/he actually made it happen.

Every time someone lets you break the safe covering of their body and risk infection for your sake, you should be not only grateful but awed by their gift. They are giving you some of the very stuff of their life. The first time someone did that for you, it was your mother, and it created you. This is a sacred communion, even if it's not sexual but merely the gift of a friend. Treat it as such.

You should take into account not only your donor's physical well-being throughout such an operation, but also their emotional well-being. Are they completely comfortable with the idea? Are they feeling well—not too tired, or stressed, or ill? Have they eaten already? Do they trust you? Sometimes it's hard for people to say no when they know that their vampire wants it. Try to remain empathically open to them, and be sure that they are really in shape for it. Perhaps treating them to a relaxing massage first might help. Creating sacred space, whether that means invoking quarters, or walking a protective circle, or lighting candles, can help them feel safer and more comfortable. (I generally let the donor help create sacred space, so they feel like an active participant rather than a passive object.) After the pricking or cutting, if they seem to be having serious discomfort, stop and attend to them, even if it means you have to quit in the middle of drinking. Make sure to give them some kind of positive body contact afterwards, and verbal appreciation helps too.

Since I'm talking about needles and blood-borne diseases, I should put in another caveat, this time about drugs—especially opiates. Most vampires that I know, including me, don't tend to be attracted to the hyperactive drugs such as cocaine or methamphetamine, since they rob us of energy; some may drink alcohol or smoke a little weed, but even these tend to annoy rather than soothe us. The one big drug that seems to be the all-time vampire favorite is opiates, whether straight opium or its more refined cousins, morphine or heroin. This is because opiates have the insidious ability to dull the prana hunger. When we're high on them, we may be starving for prana—but we don't care. We can sit at home and waste away and to hell with the whole struggle of hunting and feeding and finding new prey (or donors, if you're trying to be ethical) and dealing with survival. It's an awfully tempting fate for a tired vampire. However, trading one addiction for an even more debilitating one is not the answer.

We also tend to be rather obsessive people, and drug addictions are even more attractive to us for those reasons. If you are a vampire, please do not self-medicate with addictive drugs. I know that may be totally wasted and even ludicrous advice for those who are already on them, but for those who are just playing around, watch it. Living with a prana addiction all our lives predisposes us to think that addiction, in general, is how life should be run. After all, we reason, we as the human species are addicted to food and water and air, and we spend an inordinate amount of our time and energy securing the proper daily amounts of these, or at least the means to secure them. Why not extend this line of thinking to heroin, or soap operas, or love affairs, or whatever else you can become addicted to in order to take your mind off your life and your needs?

The line to be drawn here is one of survival. What do you really need to survive and be reasonably happy, and is there some less destructive way to get your needs met? In the end, merely palliative addictions will run you down. Also, part of being a vampire is having a part to play in the human ecosystem, a part that is both necessary and unavoidable. Distraction-addictions take you further away from life, not closer to it.

Blood Rite

The nondenominational energy-feeding ritual for lovers in Chapter 3 can be adapted for a sanguinarian pre-feeding ritual. Alternately, those wanting a more Pagan slant can use this rite.

Set up a large space in the center of your ritual area, and four candles in the primary directions. Have all your equipment ready, including first aid items. The quarters can be called by the vampire, or the donor, or someone else. The East quarter should be done by whoever will do the cutting; the others are negotiable.

East: Spirits of Air, bless this blade and make it sharp and keen. Bless my hands, and keep them steady. Purify us that no harm may come through uncleanliness.

South: Spirits of Fire, bless us with the iron will of red Mars. May we taste that iron in the scarlet flow of life. May power flow between us.

West: Spirits of Water, bless us with the salt of the inner sea, from which we came and which we hear inside us. Bless the ebb and flow of the life force between us.

North: Spirits of Earth, bless this act of nourishment and generosity, passed from one hand to the other. Even as you nourish us, we give of ourselves to each other in your example.

Center: We call upon Shiva the Destroyer, and Kali Ma who destroys him in turn. We call upon Lilith, mother of vampires. We call upon Inanna who journeys to the underworld, and Ereshkigal who welcomes her. We call upon Morrigan, Stormcrow who drinks the blood of battles. Bless us and keep us safe!

Both parties move to the center of the space, and the donor gets comfortable.

Vampire: I ask for a gift of some of your abundant life. I will receive it with gratitude and honor the wonder of your open hands. In return, I will do (some personal favor, decided by the people in question) for you. Do you consent?

Donor: I will give some of the tide of my life to you, and I will accept your gift in return. I trust you not to wound me deeply. Come and drink!

The cutting is made, by whichever individual prefers to do it, and the vampire receives blood. The aftercare commences, and when the donor is rested, both parties dismiss the elements. If desired, any burnable material (such as tissue or cloth bandages) that has blood on it can be burned as an offering at this time to the deities whose blessing was asked.

8
Healing the World

As I've said before, I don't believe that God/dess makes junk. S/he created predators and scavengers, hunters and carrion eaters, in the natural, physical ecosystem; why is it so strange that the human-psychic ecosystem should mirror this pattern? As above, so below; the longer I live, the more I see that everything is mirrored in a macrocosm-microcosm design. I also believe that we are given our gifts for a purpose, and that purpose is to use them as wisely as we can for the benefit of the world. It's all right to get what you need, but the world does not revolve around you. If our natures are a gift, not a curse, then we should be able to use them to help others. And we can.

LESSON #5: Learn to be useful to the world. I first realized our purpose when I began working with my wife, who worked with energy healing. Together we discovered that we make a good team for certain cases—bringing people down out of panic attacks, bad trips, hysteria, and other such situations. We worked out a system: with the person's permission, I stood behind them, touching lightly, and sucked out the negative stuff. She stood in front of them, holding their hands and their attention, and pumped in positive, healing energy as fast as I took the bad stuff out. We practiced together long enough for me to know when to stop.

Since then, I've worked with my second partner who is a massage therapist and practitioner of Reiki, Shiatsu, and various other healing arts. Again, he generally holds their attention as he puts positive energy into them, and I try not to draw attention to myself. Our placement in these interactions is carefully chosen. Some people, as I said before, react to deepfeeding as if it is a violation every time, even if they've consciously consented and it's being done to help them. Also, a feeding vampire's energy is not exactly soothing and nurturing; it's more like that of a junkie shooting up. A freshly fed vampire is hyperactive, bouncy, and lots of fun, but decidedly uncomfortable if you're distressed. Working as a team with a healer who can distract the client from what's going on at the back door helps to calm the client a great deal. I'd like to see more vampire-healer teams working together in the magical community; I think we could do a lot of good.

Another thing that I do is to work with my friends, and sometimes clients who are comfortable with me and trust me, to help them eliminate phobias. The method we've worked out is simple: The individual with the phobia faces the object of their fear, not necessarily up close, but at a safe distance, so that their fear level is strong but not yet overwhelming. I feed on them—often just by holding or touching them while they go through it—until they can report their fear levels significantly decreased even though they're still close to the fear object. Then we stop; there's a temptation to go on, but it is not a good idea to pull too much energy out of an already rattled individual. The next time, they can usually go a little further towards it, and it'll take more contact with the fear object to provoke the same amount of fear, which I eat. I've managed to help a lot of people this way.

When it comes to healing techniques, there is a pretty clear division between primary and secondary vampires. By our very nature, we primary vampires can handle negative energy that no one else can deal with comfortably, but we are also extremely limited in what we can do, energy-wise. I had a primary vampire friend who referred to it as being "a one-trick pony, but I can do that one trick really, really well."

Some primary vampires are fairly good at helping with physical pain, at least temporarily. One vampire said that nausea tasted good and was quite "edible" psychically, and that in order to find where someone was hurting she needed only to run her hands over their body and find the spot that "tasted" best. However, keep in mind that this is not healing the problem. It's pain relief, and nothing more, and if the individual is already weakened, it can do more harm than good. Talk to them in depth about their physical situation, and check their aura to see how "full" it is. It may be better for them to take a pill-type painkiller than to be severely depleted in a time of physical weakness.

How long the pain relief lasts will vary widely. If the situation is an ongoing injury—for example, a freshly broken bone—it may be only minutes before it all comes back. The pain may come on so quickly and intensely that it never alleviates no matter how much you take, like a leaky bowl that just keeps refilling with water. Generally, if I count ten deep breaths while feeding and the pain isn't any better, then it may not be something that I can relieve without depleting them. In the case of low-grade ongoing pain, like a back problem, I can sometimes give relief up to a couple of hours. However, don't let the individual keep coming back to you for such aid too many times; think of yourself as a severe remedy that should be reserved for emergencies.

Another use for this technique is to bring people down out of bad drug experiences, especially from hallucinogens. Sometimes people have bad trips, and regardless of how you feel about their actually taking said substances, it's ethical to help out when someone is suffering even if you don't approve of how they got that way. Be warned, however; the energy of people who are experiencing hallucinogenic drugs can be rather bad-tasting, especially if they are man-made drugs rather than natural ones. There's also the fact that an individual on a bad trip may fight you if you try to feed off of them; the drug experience may interfere with their ability to trust you, and to reason that you are not attempting to harm them. If this happens, just let it go; it's better not to force them.

Anxiety is one of the easiest energies to suck and out and remove cleanly, and have it stay removed for a good while. We've also had success bringing people out of psychotic freakouts, but it's a lot harder if the person has bad brain chemistry. Generally, if the individual is mentally fragile, one should be exceptionally careful about deepfeeding. It may feel easy and natural to you, but it is actually a pretty invasive and serious process. While fishing around in their aura, you may hit all sorts of things that can make their mood worse, so go slowly and cautiously, and be prepared to pull back if they become upset. It is extremely unsafe to use the "malocchio", or hypnotic eye, on someone who is mentally unstable, because you can knock them over the edge.

How do I tell if someone is too unstable to work on? Look at their aura, and concentrate on their third eye. If they have consented to let you touch their aura psychically, check out that third eye with an energy "tentacle". There's something in that area which resembles a "handle". Grab it, gently, and tug. The individual may actually move forward a little as you do that. (They may also react violently, so be delicate.) If the "handle" feels "loose", or seems to jiggle in your tentacle, let go and don't mess with them. They are too mentally unstable, and thus too psychically precarious, to feed from. I've never actually made someone's "handle" come loose, or torn it off (although the idea does come horrifyingly to mind), so I don't know what could happen or if it could be done, and frankly I don't intend to find out.

Exercise J: *Put the news around that as soon as a friend hurts themselves, you want to come over and work on them. Tell them not to tell you where they were hurt; run your hands over their aura and try to figure it out. Go slowly, and look for spots that seem to draw you. Alternatively, have a friend find someone you don't know who has an injury (not something obvious, like a cast on a broken leg) who is willing to take part in the experiment, and go see them with no prior knowledge of their malady. Try to identify, from their aura, where their injury is located, and what its nature is. Have someone else who has done energy work around to second-guess you. That way you can get a second opinion as to whether you got it right.*

Exercise K: *Tell your friends that if one of them is angry about something irrational and wants a break from the anger, they should come to you, because you need the practice. Defusing anger is a good thing to learn. Start by having them sit or pace across the room from you. Tell them to dwell on whatever is making them angry, and to ignore you. Loud ranting about the subject is a good distraction. Extend your tentacles or whatever you use as psychic extensions and sink them into their aura. Try to drain off the energy. They may instinctively move closer to you as you do this, as it can inadvertently "reel them in". They should be briefed to tell you when they* *feel like their anger has dissipated, and they should let you know afterwards what it felt like, and how*

If you can't seem to get a good connection with them a distance away, have them move closer. Keep in mind, however, that you may need to employ this technique in an emergency, when someone around is angry and dangerously violent, and you will probably be doing that from a line-of-sight distance. You will also be trying to do it without them noticing you, even on an unconscious level (which can happen; they may not understand what it is that you're doing, but something about you makes them uncomfortable, and they may lash out). Practice eating your friends' anger with their permission, but while they're distracted. You may want another friend to create a distraction for you. If they don't feel it even after being warned it's going to happen, then you've developed a deft enough touch to use it in emergencies as a self-defense tool. It's one of the very few times that I think it's acceptable to feed without permission.

Of course, healing is where secondary vampires really shine, if they try. A secondary vampire is automatically experienced at moving energy around between people. If they can pull it out, they can put it back. Secondary vampires can very quickly become adept at such techniques as Reiki, or Ch'i Gong, or other systems of energy healing. I strongly recommend that they do so, since it's real handy to be able to fix up your own donors. It can also be a fair trade for healing—"I help you out now, you help me out when you're feeling fully recovered and I'm feeling low." This is one place where secondary vampires have it all over primary ones; we primary ones can't always do outflow, and when we do our energy sometimes feels "wrong" or "icky". A secondary vampire can not only put out what they take in, they can fine-tune that energy to take on a particular flavor. This trick is often developed through feeding; if you experience energy in many "flavors", you'll be better at sending out a particular "flavor". A secondary vampire can work as part of a vampire-healer team, or if they're well-trained enough, they can be the vampire-healer team, all by themselves.

However, secondary vampires are just as vulnerable to the effects of negative energy flow as any non-vampire. If you are a secondary vampire who does healing by pulling negative energy out of someone, you need to do regular cleansing exercises, such as the one below. If you do a lot of pulling off of other people, you can absorb their feelings, ideas, and fears. Primary vampires can usually process the energy quickly and toss off the personal "stain", often without being conscious of it. Sometimes, however, especially if they are pulling off of one specific person for a long time (like a lover), a little can rub off. Secondary vampires are much more likely to collect rub-off. If you go long enough with cleansing, you can suddenly find yourself having thoughts, emotions (especially fears), memories, and even dreams that are not your own, and don't connect with any experience of yours. This can be pretty disorienting, and frankly, no one needs this kind of collected residue. If you feed regularly, cleanse periodically. Cleansing does use up energy, but you'll be mentally healthier.

Exercise L: *Lay flat on the earth, in a place with actual ground—not the floor of a third-floor apartment. You can lay face up, although I prefer face down, but make yourself as flat as possible. Pull the earth energy up into you. Don't worry about bringing it up through your chakras; if you're a secondary psychic vampire, you should be able to pull with your whole body and aura, letting it flow up into you like a wave. (Primary vampires may have trouble with this exercise. Keep practicing.) Hold it in you for the count of ten breaths, and with each breath let it "slosh around" inside you. Don't let it become still and quiet; I find deep breathing helps it keep moving. Visualize it washing out all the accumulated grime that you've been taking into yourself. If you like, picture it concentrating on stuff that isn't yours, that you pulled out of others. Fill your lungs with air, hold it for a count of ten, and then let it out. At the same time, let the energy all run out of you, back into the ground. You'll feel somewhat drained afterwards, but it's good to do it periodically for purposes of keeping yourself from getting "gunked up".*

One technical energy-healing skill that can usually be learned by any psychic vampire is psychic surgery. By this I am not referring to the sort of thing that is claimed by some alleged psychic healers—that they can reach into someone and physically remove a tumor or a blockage. My jury is still out on whether that can be done, and even if it can, the vast majority of people who claim to be able to do it are quacks.

Actual psychic surgery is the ability to reach into someone and suck the life out of whatever is ailing them. If, for example, they have a localized bacterial infection, the idea is to suck the life out of the offending bacteria while not harming the surrounding cells. This takes great talent at being able to see and/or sense where the difficulty is, and those who want to try this ought to get some good training in energy healing of the sort where diagnosis is stressed. On top of this, you need to learn to extrude your energy in very delicate, narrow tendrils (or claws, or threads, or whatever seems most natural for you to envision). You need to learn to use them to surgically pinpoint the cells to be drained, and not mess with healthy tissues. Psychic surgery can't be crude, or it will do the client more harm than good.

Teaching is another good profession where the magnetism of a healthy vampire can charm and inspire students, and the vampire will be well-fed, because he can get the juice from them. Sarah Dorrance writes: "I teach partly because I love English and English literature, and partly because I love the rapt attention students give me when I lecture and tutor. The energy I put into my teaching is more than returned by the time my hour at the podium is over. Every time I've lectured, I've come out of that experience as high as a kite. I love, and need, the energy I am given."

Music, of course, has long been a mainstay of vampires who have some kind of performance talent, because music can be a great mind-alterer. If you perform the right sort of music—and it's less about the genre than about the quality of the performance—you can get people into an open, receptive mood where they will give forth energy in the form of emotions. Performing is always an activity that skirts the boundaries of ethics; by its own nature, performance is always manipulative. However, the people who show up for it are implicitly consenting to be manipulated; they expect to be "made" to feel something—joy, humor, sorrow, fear, empathy—and thus it is not unethical to take what you can, as long as they leave feeling satisfied with your performance. For such a situation, we're generally talking lightfeeding anyway; you can't dip deeply into someone while you're busy doing your thing up on stage.

However, performance can be used as a form of energy healing, if you're careful, canny, and know your audience extremely well. This does, however, require that the vampire in question put themselves in harm's way, as it were. The process of trying this trick is as follows:

1. This works best when the subject matter of the performance is something controversial, and something that you believe in strongly, so that you can project real sincerity.

2. You get your audience uncomfortable, but not too alienated. This is a fine line, and you'd better be very careful not to screw up. Practice on friends first.

3. You feed on the negative emotion swirling around them. Take as much of it as you can. This is where you should stuff yourself. The more you can drain out of the atmosphere, the better.

4. You then alleviate their discomfort by changing the focus from challenging or confronting them to reassuring them, perhaps stressing the positive side of your subject, or addressing fears compassionately, or creating empathy. This creates positive energy to fill up the void that you created.

Why bother to turn the energy to something positive? Why not just stir them up to a froth of angst until they storm out? Well, first of all, they didn't come there to be made upset. It's not a good thing to toy with them and then drop them. Besides, if they come out better, they'll remember it as a good experience, and they might want to come back. They'll also remember your subject matter positively, which can be pretty important. Doing this trick can, in small groups, actually be a lot like a mild version of the phobia treatment described above. Never underestimate the power of a dedicated vampire with a higher mission than just their next meal.

9
The Wyrd and the Darkness:
Gods and Spirituality

Dark as the womb, as the night, as the cave,
Peace like the tomb and the deep open grave,
And you wonder how much of yourself will be saved
When your soul goes under her knife...

Her garden the graveyard, her passion the storm,
Her love is as deep as the void without form,
Her kiss is the taste of sweet blood on the knife,
For out of the darkness comes life...

–From *Song For The Dark Goddess* RKaldera 2001

If you've even read this far in the book, it can be assumed that you
are willing to accept things that are not usually accepted. It might even
be guessed that you are following some sort of spiritual path, or are at
least searching for one. As a Neo-Pagan shaman, I work with a
polytheistic path, but I realize not everyone else does or should. My
statements on spirituality are not meant to assert that the Neo-Pagan
path is right for everyone, or for every vampire; it is merely the road I
am most familiar with. Treading down that road, I have found a lot of
useful answers. If they work for you, great. If not, keep searching; when
we spread out we can cover more ground.

Many of the vampires that I interviewed for this book were not
Pagan, and were perfectly happy in their religious choices. One
Episcopalian vampire commented that "in addition to my exotic
lovemaking practices, I also feed once a week at the communion rail ...
I get lost in life, in the flowing pulse or love itself. My soul wants to
drown itself in a river of warm, enveloping love and life. That's what it
feels like when I drink. It is Communion. It is more Communion than
what I took at the altar rail as a teenager, hoping that something would

happen but not knowing what it was that I was waiting for." (This brings us to the additional point that any energetically charged item, from a communion wafer to someone's athame, can be a source of prana to feed from.) Other vampires simply choose not to work their psychic talents into their spirituality at all, regarding them as no more a part of their religion than, say, an ability to run fast or hit notes with perfect pitch. Some, of course, are atheists, with no religious beliefs at all.

For those who walk the Pagan path, however, there is a niche for psychic vampires. It is not yet widely accepted, but it should be. Because they work so often with people's negative energy, vampires are frequently fascinated by death, pain, blood, and power. There's something in even the most peaceable vampire that instinctively understands the Plutonian vibration of power, despair and transformation. Those caught up in the mythic vampire archetype may like to burn black candles and put skulls on their altars. They may gravitate to lifestyles, music, clothing, imagery, and religion that are dark, morbid, connected to death and dissolution. They may have little use for the white-light-peace earthy-crunchy-granola pagans, and when they walk into covens in their black leather or black lace or black lipstick, death's heads dangling from their ears and whips dangling from their belts, people who are repelled by the aesthetic have little use for them either.

This means many vampires end up in amoral, negative magic practices, because the trappings are similar and the people don't turn them away for being what they are. However, some of those magical and religious practices have very unbalanced ethical systems that play into whatever amoral illusions a vampire uses to justify nonconsensual feeding, and they end up very nasty people with karmic debts that are way out of control. This too, does not have to happen. There is a place for that death and darkness in the Neo-Pagan path. We have patron deities who will respond to our needs, if we become—at least to some extent—their tools of transformation.

I strongly believe in the power of karma, that what we do does come back to us, that what we put out is what we get back, that what we sow we shall reap. You may disagree with this idea. If so, you should probably stop reading now, because the rest of this chapter is predicated on the existence of that Law of Return. I also believe that it is especially important for vampires to keep a close eye on our karma. If we aren't careful, we may end up doing a lot of harm that we didn't mean to do. None of us are perfect—including me—and we do slip up from time to time. We have to work to keep from slipping up, using the discipline that we work out for ourselves, and we also have to work at putting enough good back into the world to make up for our slippage. There, I've used the word "work" three times in one sentence. That ought to drive the point home that we were not put here to follow an easy road. However, another one of my idealistic beliefs that has proven itself true over the course of time is that greater trials mean greater rewards.

In the Neo-Pagan worldview (at last as I experience it), the gods of the Underworld, of death/rebirth and the dark places within, are the sternest ones of all. They do not suffer fools. They do not tolerate laziness. They have no patience with snot-nosed cases of arrested emotional development. They eat blenders for lunch. Their path is the hardest of all, because there is no leeway, no room for mistakes, and it is also incredibly valuable. The lessons that they teach us can literally change our entire lives, transforming us into different people.

Many of the deities presented below were traditionally invoked with a blood offering, if only a drop of one's own blood let fall from the fingertip. I've found that this invokes them faster and stronger than any other offering, and they seem to appreciate it more. Women can use menstrual blood; the wise "moon blood" does belong to the Crone phase of the lunar goddess, as every bleeding is technically a life that did not come to fruition. However, if you shed blood as part of a ritual to invoke or honor any of these deities, please follow the blood safety rules in Chapter 7 so as not to harm yourself or another. Be sure that anything you bleed onto gets burned, or buried in the earth, or kept in a safe place where no one else can find it. Remember that with blood offerings, as with sanguinarian feedings, a very little amount goes a very long way.

Treating blood like hazardous waste (which you should do) may seem somehow disrespectful to its sacred nature, but please keep in mind that in ancient cultures, the line between "holy" and "taboo" was very thin and possibly even nonexistent. Think of blood shed during a magical ritual as something very magically powerful, so much so that it might strongly affect anyone who touches it. It might also dishonor the deity you have offered it to, if other people were handling or walking on it. Use the safety guidelines with this mindset rather than thinking of it as "filthy" or "diseased".

One deity who has long been associated with vampires is the Sumerian goddess Lilith. In her original myth, she lives in a huluppu tree between a dragon at the roots and an eagle at the height, between earth and air. This position reminds us of our constant need to balance the nourishment of the physical body with the hunger for prana; we vampires live our lives poised between the needs of earth and the needs of air. If we move closer to one than to the other, we suffer. Lilith is driven out of her tree by Gilgamesh, who has orders from Inanna the Queen of Heaven to evict the tenants and cut down the tree to make furniture for her. Lilith flees into the desert, becoming the personification of the scirrocco and the barren sands.

In Hebrew myth, she is the first wife of Adam, evicted from Eden for her lack of submissive behavior. During medieval times, her legend grew until she was a feared demon of sex and death, killing babies in the cradle, climbing into bed between a couple and making them both barren with her love. She birthed a veritable army of small androgynous demons that sucked the life force out of people; in their male form they were called incubi, and in their female form succubi. A succubus might lie with a man in his sleep, causing wet dreams, and then turn herself into an incubus and fertilize a sleeping woman with his seed. Lilith and her demonic children visited their prey over and over again, slowly draining them of life-force until they died. These creatures do seem to fit the profile of the psychic vampire far closer than the blood-drinking myth, although they are overladen with centuries of a near-hysterical fear of sex.

If we scrape away the years of medieval sex-negativity, we find Lilith to be a strong goddess who is associated with sex and death. In some Talmudic traditions, the children that she murders in the cradle would have grown up to be evil people, and her efforts keep down the number of violent criminals in the world. This echoes the attraction we vampires have to strong, harmful emotions in others, emotions that we devour and destroy. Lilith was associated with the Queen of Sheba in her guise as the Asker Of Hard Questions; she loves to point out the flaws in people's plans and excuses and prevarications. In a group of people where so much is still underground and so little is conscious and honest, we need Lilith's ambivalent blessing more than ever.

Lilith is also a goddess of lust, reaffirming the concept that sexuality is in itself a holy and powerful force. Whether primary or secondary, it's nearly impossible to find a vampire who isn't drawn by sexual energy. Prana-feeding itself, whether from aura or blood, can be a profoundly spiritual experience as well. This is especially true when it is done with a long-time familiar partner with a good knowledge of magic and energy flows; it can become a very intense form of sex magic if done right.

> Lovemaking is a way to reach a higher spiritual plane; the God within me recognizes and salutes and worships the God within my lover. We all have God within us; if more of us were aware of this at all times, we'd be a lot less cruel to each other as a species, I suspect. The intimacy of drinking blood is blinding. It is such an affirmation of love (and what is God but love itself?) and life that it can drown you.
>
> —Sarah Dorrance

In Hindu belief, the god Shiva the Destroyer is mythically associated with vampires. Unlike his co-trinitarians Brahma and Vishnu, Shiva can be appealed to by those who have no status in caste-conscious Hindu society, such as vampires, demons, untouchables, beggars, mendicants, hermits, and ascetics. Shiva dances the sacred dance Tandava while holding a skull in each hand; it symbolizes the neverending cycle of death and rebirth and death again. His worshippers have been known to meet in cremation grounds, and keep human skulls as reminders of the essential impermanence of everything but that cycle.

Shiva is both a slayer of and a patron of vampires and demons. This may seem contradictory, but it makes sense when taking in the ascetic, disciplined nature of his character. When he is not dancing, he is most often shown meditating on a mountaintop, seeking enlightenment through rigorous practice. His goal in this meditation is to achieve the obliteration of all Illusion, and he holds his devotees to this goal as well. The difference between the vampires and demons that he slays and the ones that he defends is this: For the latter group, spiritual discipline is a part of their life, and illusions are not. For the former group, it is reversed.

Vampires can find yet another similarity in Shiva the Destroyer; he is the god who drinks and transforms poison. When the great serpent Vasuki threatened to kill the world by spewing venom over it, Shiva placed his mouth against the serpent's jaws and drank all the poison as fast as it came out. He transmuted it into pure water with the power of his own body, and although his throat was burned blue with the effort, the world was saved. This is a perfect metaphor for what we do when we use vampiric powers to unburden others of their pain and neutralize it. Certain Native American tribes referred to this as "snake medicine", and those who were masters could literally take snake venom into their bodies and make it harmless by the power of their own will. Shiva's treatment of Vasuki—which renders the serpent harmless but does not kill it—echoes this ability. Shiva wears the serpent around his neck now, living proof that there is nothing that cannot be cured.

Shiva has four spouses, all of whom are both separate deities and also aspects of the same goddess Shakti, who is Shiva's female side. These are Uma the innocent maiden, Parvati the wife and mother and dancer, Durga the warrior and comrade in arms, and Kali, who does to Shiva what he does to everyone else. It is Kali with whom we must deal next, as she is the Lady of Blood. Kali is dark-skinned, representing the darkness of the earth; she is often shown emaciated and wild, with her tongue extended in an audacious salute. Skulls hang around her neck, and her skirts are made of thighbones. Her belt is a string of severed hands, symbolizing that all the works of the world are powerless against her. In one of her four hands she holds a sword; in another a severed head. Her other two hold a lotus blossom and make the mudra of "Be not afraid", meaning that we should not fear Death.

She births life and then consumes it, the Creative and Devouring Mother in one being. Sometimes she is portrayed as sitting on the passive Shiva's erect penis while she simultaneously devours his guts. This is more than a bizarre sexual scenario; it is symbolic of her role as She Who Births and She Who Slays in one. Vampires who study her learn to realize that no one is all-destroyer or all-powerful; those who take must also give, and those who are powerful must in turn learn to be humble and submit.

Like Shiva, cremation grounds are her sacred places. Also like Shiva, Kali can be called upon to bring radical change into someone's life, but if Shiva is stern and uncompromising, Kali is harsher still. Calling her into one's life—or being visited by her—can be a dramatic and sometimes violent transition. She does not wait until someone is comfortable before turning their entire life upside down, and resistance is usually useless against her burning-ground tactics. If you are being troubled by a vampire who is addicted to unethical practices, Kali may be the one to ask for help. She does not take sides, but she will do whatever is necessary to push someone into a life-changing experience. Of course, if you ask her to help with someone else, she is likely to take an interest in you as well.

For the Babylonians, the Underworld was ruled by the dark goddess Ereshkigal. In the tale of Inanna, the Queen of Heaven travels to her sister's kingdom. Her external reason is to pay her respects at the funeral of Ereshkigal's recently dead husband. Her internal reason is that she seeks a deeper experience. When she passes through the gates of Ereshkigal's realm, she is stripped of her robes, jewelry, crown, amulets, title, and even her name. These things, she is informed, count for nothing here. Ereshkigal herself then freezes her with the Eye of Death and hangs her on the wall above her throne, a corpse on a meathook.

When Inanna does not come home, the inventor god Enki sends two androgynous people to negotiate with the Goddess of Death for Inanna's return. Rather than argue or cajole, they weep for her, shedding tears of sympathy for the pain of her destiny and her terrible job. She is so moved that she releases Inanna, who returns to the surface rebirthed and more powerful than ever after her ordeal.

Another example of Underworld-as-test-and-ordeal is the Celtic story if Pwyll, who meets with Arawn, the Lord of the Underworld in that mythos. Arawn offers to trade places with Pwyll, enchanting them both so that they will appear to be each other, for a year and a day. The catch is that Pwyll cannot sleep with Arawn's wife, in spite of her beauty and her pleas; there are hints that she is really the Black Darling, the Goddess of Death, and as such it would be death for him to treat her like a subordinate wife. It is a year-long test of Pwyll's will, as he struggles against his cultural upbringing which cries out to merely ravish her and have done with it. When Pwyll honorably completes his year and goes back to his own tribe, he discovers that Arawn has ruled so wisely and well that he must now live up to his example.

One thing that we vampires can be very good at, if we try, is arranging cathartic ordeals for other people. Mature vampires, who have spent many years experiencing (of only briefly) the pain and fear of others have a good sense of what pushes which buttons. We can transmute this knowledge into an ability to create ordeal-oriented rituals for other people. Of course, ordeal rituals only work when the individual consents, and indeed strongly desires such an experience for their own personal self-knowledge. We must never fall into the trap of assuming we know what is best for others, as it is all too easy to hide our hunger behind this kind of egotism.

It's why so many (although certainly not all) vampires are drawn to S/M. Creating a safe space for another person to explore their own fears and test themselves against pain is a heady experience for us—and a good feed. For those of us who do both sex magic and S/M, it is not that far a step for ritual sex to become a ritual ordeal, in which one person makes a symbolic trip to the Underworld and back, facing their own inner demons.

Of course, these rituals can also be created in nonsexual form for people who are not lovers. Vampires take easily to the theatrical ability to wear the mask of someone's demons. Often we've learned to be chameleons anyway, in order get different people's attention for feeding. Our problem in such ritual ordeals isn't that we aren't able to portray whichever stern or forbidding or cruel God of Death the initiate requires of us; it's that we need to be able to keep our own hungers and issues in the background. To be the image of a Death God for someone requires objectivity and distance, and careful attention to their state of mind. If we're underfed, this can be like being starving at a dinner table where you're expected to maintain formal manners and serve everyone else first. There's a balance to be struck between our hunger and their need; in the end, such a ritual has to be slanted towards the person taking the shaman's journey.

Ereshkigal's gift is that of the consenting cathartic ordeal that allows someone to pit themselves against their own fears and win. By using our talents of performance and the raw aggression of our hunger, we can create the atmosphere. By using our gift of removing fear (described in Chapter 8), we can aid them in this process. By learning compassion, discipline, and objectivity, we can keep from screwing it up with our own greedy survival instincts. Like a vampire, the greatest gift that Ereshkigal could be offered was someone's honest tears.

Among the Aztec pantheon of gods, the jaguar goddess Tlazolteotl is also useful to us. She is a lunar goddess, with a different personality in each of her four phases. In her new moon phase, she was seen as an adolescent, cruel and yet delightful, and totally unreliable. This aspect is eerily reminiscent of the modern mythic vampire archetype, who seems to be stuck in a permanent callous adolescence. It may be that one needs to go through this phase before one can move on to better things, if only so that one can have some compassion for those still stuck in it, and try to show a way out while speaking in language that they may understand.

In her second phase, the waxing moon, she becomes a young woman who is the patron of illicit sex and gambling. Like Lilith, she is here a goddess of lust, and recalls the strong drive toward sexual energy that we often find ourselves trapped in. (One wonders how may people who show up at Sex and Love Addicts Anonymous are actually hungry vampires whose pursuit of their favorite energy is interfering with their lives.) Her association with gambling reminds us of the kind of exciting and tormented adventures that a hungry vampire will get involved with in order to get fed.

However, when the moon reaches its fullest point and then begins to wane, Tlazolteotl's character changes entirely. She is shown as a stern yet compassionate priestess whose title is "Eater of Filth". Her task is to take confessions of sins that mortals offer, and then devour those sins, along with their anger and hatred and fear. She opens festering psychic wounds and devours their infections, allowing sufferers to heal cleanly. In her aspect as the Eater of Filth, she brings blessings to marriages and the home. It is this transformation, from careless adventurer to responsible priestess, that brings home the karmic task of a vampire. Tlazolteotl's job is so clearly ours as well; we too can bring peace to others by receiving their wounds and devouring what we find there. Ideally, this is the proper evolution for us.

In her fourth face, that of the dark moon, Tlazolteotl embodies the Dark Goddess in her form as Fury, bringing a harsh justice to wrongdoers and avenging victims. She is the Jaguar Goddess, who leaps and rends them with fang and claw. Although this role may look appealing, keep in mind that it occurs only after she has been the Eater of Filth for some time. One cannot go from heartless adolescent to dark avenger; that role is reserved for those who have learned compassion and healing. Those who try to skip the all-important third phase will find themselves caught up in a delusion of being a Fury, and they will do a great deal of damage. A sense of true justice cannot come out of self-centeredness; it must be an equal balance of self-knowledge and empathy for others.

The deity to whom I am personally sworn is the Norse goddess of the dead, whose name may be the most invoked of any Pagan god. She is called Hel, and the Christian afterworld was named for her, although her realm has very little in common with it. In Norse mythos, Hel collects all the ordinary dead, as opposed to the select few warriors that go to the halls of Odin or Freya. She manifests in many different forms, but her most hideous is that of a woman who is half blue as death and half rotting corpse. She is stern and quiet, moving slowly and speaking only in important truths.

Her legend lived on in post-heathen times as the *draugr* or *aptrganger*, vampires who were "blue as death" and had powers of shapeshifting and controlling the weather. Hel's mother, the witch-giantess Angrboda the Hag of the Iron Wood, lived on in myths of Black Annis, the hag who drinks blood in the Dane Hills of Leicestershire, England. Although the werewolf is not within the scope of this book, they are often found alongside of vampires in legend, and Hel's brother is the great werewolf Fenris. The Iron Wood, where Hel and her siblings were born, is rife with members of the Nordic giant-race who are werewolves, vampires, and shapeshifting trolls.

Hel is a good goddess to invoke for those who are having trouble with the physical reality of death, or who are caught up in the glamour of some myth of immortality. As implied by her image, she does not flinch from showing people the reality of death, and that it is part of the cycle for everyone. Hel is very good for bringing arrogant people down to earth, as it were.

Perhaps this is the place to interject another odd talent that seems to turn up regularly in vampires: Many have a strange affinity with the weather, especially violent weather. I started playing with minor weather magic as a child (with disastrous results). I've also interviewed many other vampires who can tell when storms are coming, or who dream about storms and then discover that a huge one struck in another part of the world while they slept. Those who can draw off of non-living sources often find that the air before and during a storm is especially useful in that regard. One could theorize that when you have a skill—instinctive or learned—for moving energy around, you naturally start feeling weather shifts as patterns of energy much like that in a body. In a sense, the weather is the prana in the Earth's aura, and weather patterns are her energy meridians. Those vampires who find it difficult to draw off of Her body directly might well find storms easier to work with; I've met a few who were actually "stormchasers", following tornadoes perilously closely for the adrenaline rush ... or is it the energy contained in them?

There's also the fact that storm gods are often death gods in many cultures. In the Afro- Caribbean Yoruba tradition, the goddess of both weather and death is Oya, the volatile trickster goddess who may bless you one moment and smash you the next. Her favorite offerings are purple fruits and vegetables, such as plums, eggplants, and red wine. The Irish goddess Morrigan, lady of storm and battle, inspired heroes to do great deeds in her service and then collected their souls from the battlefield. She was associated with crows and ravens, whose alternative name "blood-goose" shows their carrion-eating, blood-drinking side. Since she was also the muse of poets, writing a poem in her honor might be a good way to win her momentary favor.

I don't, in general, advocate messing with the weather too much. I've had too many terrible results to recommend it. Weather patterns are like a big chain that wraps around the globe, and extends backwards in time and forwards into probability. If you yank on that chain, assuming you get results at all, you will get more results than you expect, and many of them may be much worse than you wanted. You will also affect a lot of other people who have to live under the same sky that you do. Instead, I strongly suggest that you make an offering to a storm deity and ask them for help. If you can feed off of storms, do it; it's free, and the Earth has plenty to spare in Her aura. Just be safe; stay under some kind of cover, and don't go pointing swords up at the sky on hilltops during lightning storms, as so many cute pagan books unfortunately illustrate.

The responsibilities of a priest/ess of the Dark Gods are many—caring for the dying and their survivors, for the mentally ill, for would-be suicides; neo-pagan funerals and mourning rites for divorces, and abortions and miscarriages; ritual ordeals of passage, banishings, and religious S/M. There are too many out there who talk about nurturing and community but cannot deal with a near-corpse in need of a bedpan change. Those of us who flirt with Death in our dreams and sex lives had better get serious and put out.

AA speaks of turning to a higher power, but vampires need to turn to a deeper power, one that understands dark hungers and thirsts, dark desires, who can take you down to your depths and back out again. High Priest/esses who find that a vampire has wandered in to their coven might want to point them toward the Underworld Gods and suggest they ask their wisdom. HP's should also accept this as a path as necessary as Maiden, Mother, Warrior, or Sacred King, even if the Dark Gods give them the "Wilis".

Vampires who are aware and ethical have a lot to teach—about moving energy, about accepting the dark places within. With Her blessing, perhaps we can teach the world that the end of a cycle deserves as much attention and respect as the beginning.

10
The Vampire and the Shaman

I'm not the first writer to notice that folkloric vampires and tribal shamans share similarities, especially in legends from similar parts of the world. This comparison—between the vampire archetype and the shaman archetype—has been made before, but it is still vague and confusing. There is something going on there, but there's a lot of argument as to what it is, or how deep it goes.

The folkloric vampire is not like the modern novelist's vampire. They are usually either animated corpses—and not pretty ones, either—or undead creatures who can send their souls out astrally to prey on people. In fact, the most common folkloric story of vampire attack is that of a noncorporeal creature. They consorted with unquiet ghosts, and there is much more overlap between folkloric vampires and ghosts than modern novelists' vampire portrayals. Their bodies, when exposed, lay as if dead, but did not decay. They could be "fixed" in their graves by a stake of ash or hawthorn. They must obey many strange rules and taboos in order to maintain their artificial life, such as sleeping in their native earth (straight in the ground or in a box), not seeing the sun, etc. They took on many animal shapes, such as wolves, dogs, birds, bats, cats, etc. (Although werewolves are strongly associated with vampires in folklore, they generally had only one form to shift into.) They are generally seen as impotent, although some were said to impregnate women during their sleep (merging with the myth of Lilith's incubi).

As we turn to the other archetype—which is more than just an archetype, it is a specific job performed by people all over the world, even today—I should differentiate between a "classic" shaman and a "core" shaman. The word "shamanism" has been thrown around a great deal these days, and attached to all manner of things, sometimes with only a vague understanding of its meaning. Most people who go to a class on "shamanic this-or-that" have very little knowledge of what actual tribal shamans practiced in any given cultures, or what sorts of things were and are practiced transculturally among them. A researcher or interested seeker, looking through all the widely varied literature, will notice both similarities and differences between anthropological descriptions of long-ago tribal shamans and modern-day shamanic practitioners. They may also run across specialized terms such as "core shamanism"; "shamanistic practice"; "shamanistic behavior", and so on. It can be rather confusing.

The term "core shamanism" was popularized by Michael Harner in his book *The Way Of The Shaman*. It supposedly implies that it contains the "core" shamanic techniques, stripped of their cultural context and teachable to individuals not raised in that culture. On the other hand, the experience of people who work with core shamanism is not identical to that of shamans and their counterparts who come to their work the old-fashioned way, anthropological accounts of which have been gathered for over two hundred years. There are stunning similarities between the experiences of many of these shamans, regardless of their home culture or place in the world. These similarities, and the similarities of the altered-state and magical techniques used by tribal shamans, have popularized the concept of the global "shamanic" spiritual/magical system.

I've chosen to use the term "classic shamanism" to describe the cross-cultural set of experiences described by tribal shamans across the world. It shares with "core shamanism" many of the same tools and techniques of consciousness—journeying, visualization, drumming, ritual, working with animal and plant totems, natural spirits, or ancient gods; natural hallucinogens, cultural symbol systems, and so forth. It isn't the tools that differentiate the two, as core shamanism borrowed those tools from classic shamanism. Instead, it's the central spiritual experience that is strongly different..

To be clear, however: Not all shamans in traditional tribal societies follow the "classic shaman" pattern. For example, among the Jivaro Indians, as many as a quarter of the men in the tribe may be trained as shamans, and the knowledge can be bought for the fee of a gun and some ammunition. This would make most of them analogous to "core shamans". In other tribal societies, a shaman's son or daughter may be trained in the position; sometimes they are chosen before birth with divination methods (which would suggest spirit-choosing, like the classic experience) and sometimes they are merely selected by their parent when old enough. In some areas of the world, where the tradition has all but died out, a member of the tribe may volunteer to take on the work whether or not they have been contacted by the spirits, in order to keep the tradition alive.

A classic shaman's experience is marked by the following:

1. A death-and-rebirth experience. This is not the sort of religious "born-again" fervor of a convert. This nearly always comes with a severe physical illness that brings the shaman literally to the point of death. It is often accompanied by a psychotic break. After this experience, the shaman is not only sane, but usually one of the most emotionally stable people in the tribe. However, the spirit initiation could take months, and was incredibly dangerous and harrowing. The key hallucination, which seems to be prevalent among classic shamans worldwide, is that of being dismembered and rebuilt differently.

2. In some cultures, once the shaman had passed through his ordeals and looked as if he was going to make it, he was literally buried in a grave and allowed to "rise", symbolizing his condition. In other tribes, the village was shown a dummy of the shaman's corpse, and were told that he was dead, while he is actually secreted in a hut or in the wilderness. In some traditions, such as those of northern Europe, a shaman is literally referred to as a "walking dead man". One modern classic shaman that I know commented that the question wasn't as to whether he had actually died, it was about whether he had actually come back all the way ... to which the answer was No.

3. The death-and-rebirth experience involves a great deal of astral body modification, which is dramatic and permanent. Some—not all— classic shamans are said to look like a reanimated corpse astrally. This experience is usually nonconsensual; the individual did not choose to be a shaman, they were chosen by the gods and spirits. Once the shaman has come through the other side of the change, they can never go back.

They must continue their shamanic duties for the rest of their lives, or their illness will recur and lead to insanity or death.

4. After this rebirth, which has a high attrition rate—many die, or go mad, or are otherwise wrecked by the experience—the shaman finds that they can speak to spirits and gods, and otherwise has extraordinary powers. These powers do not leap forth full-blown, however; usually a great deal of training needs to be put in. Much of this training is done by the gods and spirits themselves; a human mentor is necessary to pass on information and symbol systems, but otherworldly beings do the lion's share of the training.

5. There are different kinds of shamans; some are healers who use their powers to "suck" illnesses and evil spirits out of people. Others work with the dead, the spirits, and the gods to deliver messages and divine the future. Shamans are frequently known to hang out with the ghosts of tribal ancestors, in order to propitiate them or lay them to rest. They generally have a strong connection to land-spirits, whom they consult in order to help the tribe with agricultural pursuits. Some require the proximity of their tribal ground—and its attendant land-spirit—for maximum magical power.

6. Shamans frequently travel to other realms astrally, sending out their astral forms. This is referred to as "journeying" among modern Pagans, or "faring forth" among Norse/Germanic seidhr-workers. New Agers still tend to refer to it as "the out-of-body experience". During this period, the shaman's body lies as if inert, while his form can go to various places, but especially the Land of the Dead.

7. While a shaman is bound to serve a tribe, he does not always have to be ethical to those outside his tribe. There are legends of shamans who were able to project themselves astrally and attack or feed on enemies of the tribe. The Saami people, among others, had traditions of shamans with long-distance vampiric powers.

8. Taboos play a great role in the lives of classic shamans. For every power given to them by the spirits, they must pay with some lifelong taboo regarding clothing, food, or behavior. Their lives become entirely bounded and restricted with strange rules, through which they are able

to gain power. The shaman's relationship with the gods and spirits, unlike that of the magician, is as their servant, or at best their equal, but never their master.

9. Shamans often shapeshift astrally into other animals in order to travel places quickly on the astral plane. Their animal forms are quite varied, and most have several forms that they can use. This is different from modern "shifters" who generally only work with one totem or shape.

10. Once they gained their place in the tribe, many shamans did not marry or have children. There were exceptions to this rule (especially in cultures where the shamanic talents were passed through a family line), but it was often said that it was bad for someone to marry a shaman, due to psychic stresses caused by being in proximity to their magic. Some shamans were considered bereft of blood ties; they had no family, they were dead to their blood kin, but they were now related to the entire tribe that they were to serve. All the children of the tribe were their children; all the people were their kin, and none.

11. In some cultures, future shamans were said to be born with teeth—the *taltos*, for example, is a legendary Hungarian shaman-figure who is born with a full set of teeth and eats raw flesh from birth.

As is probably apparent from reading this list, there is a huge amount of overlap between vampire lore and shamanic lore. In both cases, the archetype is set apart from the ordinary life of humanity by undergoing a death-and-rebirth, and all the various consequences that this entails. Vampires are also associated with shapeshifting, taboos, and so forth. This is not to say that just because classic vampires and classic shamans share folklore that a vampire is a shaman or vice versa. The truth, I expect, is far more complicated and convoluted than that. My reasons for examining these archetypes together are twofold: first, there are too many coincidences for close comfort, and second, the issue strikes home for me. I am both a psychic vampire and a shaman.

In comparing these archetypes, however, one strong difference becomes clear: the shaman is in service to a tribe of people, while the vampire is a parasite who gives nothing back. While the shaman archetype did become somewhat sinister after centuries of repression of tribal religions, shamans were originally some of the most respected people in their tribes. Some did physical healing, some did psychological healing—the sort of thing that people utilize therapy for today—and some mediated between human and divine or ancestral powers. I'm not in a position to tell psychic vampires of any stripe what to do with their lives, but I have always believed that what one gives out comes back. If nothing else, the shaman archetype teaches that even a walking dead man can serve the living, and pay for the extension on his life. Similarly, a vampire can pay for the energy that she takes from others by attaching herself to a group of people that she cares about, and helping them with whatever gifts she has been given.

A shaman without a tribe will generally be assigned one by the gods and spirits that he serves. If he refuses the order, his second life is taken from him and he dies again, this time permanently. A vampire who is too solitary, who uses his nature as a way to isolate himself from others, ends up with an empty, shallow, selfish life. Embracing the Dark may be necessary, and even laudatory, but eventually one has to come up into the light and share what has been learned.

Prayer For A Vampire Shaman

For behold, I am dead, yet I live!

My flesh has touched the Ancestors
And returned to serve my descendants.
My soul has been dismembered
And rebuilt by the Will of the Gods.
My mind has been torn apart
And reconstructed by the hands of the spirits.
My heart has been ripped from me

And replaced still beating
With a strong passion for the life of this world.

I come fresh from the grave, O Mother Rot,
Your scent still on me, I walk the world
And from this death I have learned compassion.
I come fresh from the darkness, O Father Bone,
Wrapped in the hem of Your robe, I am safe
And like a seed I reach upward toward the light.
My soul is held to my body with iron bands,
That I may live once more,
Yet I know that they will be loosed again
Should I fail in my task.

My hands will reach out to the Living who cry out
And suck the poison from their bodies and minds.
My sight will reach out to the Dead who cry out
And lead them safe to their place of rebirth.
I know the Dark, it does not frighten me,
And I shall be a guide for those trapped in Your realms
Who cannot find their way out.

Show my hands where to reach, O Gods.
Show my sight where to fly, O Gods.
Show my feet where to travel, O Gods.
Let this rebirth be not wasted on selfishness.
Let this rebirth be not wasted on mourning.
Let this rebirth be a triumph
For more than just myself,
For my family, my clan, my tribe, my community
And all those who cry out, living or dead,
That my hands can draw forth from darkness.

11
Vampire Communities

As far as we can tell, most current vampire communities didn't really exist before the coming of the Internet. There were blood fetishists in the S/M and body modification/urban primitive communities, and some hung out there; there were lots of would-be vampires dancing in Goth clubs, but the Internet was what began to draw people together. Even then, it was the sanguinarians of all stripes—who couldn't exactly be unconscious of their habits—who began to advertise for others to talk to. Conscious psychic vampires began to be drawn to the groups, and arguments broke out over who deserved what label. Some sanguinarians realized that they were actually psychic vampires who chose to get their prana in large doses straight from blood, but others were doing it for other reasons and purposes and felt that this was not an accurate label for them. There were debates over, essentially, whether a sanguinarian psychic vampire had more in common with other non-psivamp blood drinkers or other non-blood-drinking psivamps.

Second Edition Note: For the definitive history of vampire communities, not to mention a lot of commentary on various aspects of them, your best bet is to check out Michelle Belanger's book *Vampires In Their Own Words*, which concisely details the rise and differentiation of various factions within the online vampire demographics. It also contains short interviews with various leaders of different sorts of vampire groups, explaining their direction.

Today there are a variety of groups that use the word "vampire". Sometimes that word is spelled "vampyre" instead; this started as a label for live human vampires as opposed to the folkloric type, but has become a term for "lifestylers" who live a life permeated with the fictional vampire archetype, regardless of whether they take part in either psychic or sanguinarian vampirism. Some vampire groups are magical/occult in nature, based on ceremonial magic, chaos magic, LaVeyan Satanism, or some combination of the above. The oldest example of this might be the Temple of Set's Order of the Vampire, which teaches psychic vampirism methods to initiates (and is generally contemptuous of all the other sorts of vampires). Another example might be House Kheperu, which teaches their own tradition of psychic/magical arts, continued in the Kherete groups. Other groups have a religious bent, usually the darker paths of Neo-Paganism but sometimes other faiths. Some are more philosophical than religious or magic-practicing. Some are simply social groups where one or more sort of vampire can congregate and get support.

Some, such as House of the Dreaming, are highly formal and ritualized. Some, like Lost Haven, reject formality and do public service. Some are based around New York nightclubs; some prefer to piggyback onto science fiction conventions. Some are long-distance and exist only online. In the past five to ten years, the number and types of groups claiming vampiric affiliations has climbed rapidly, as various demographics find each other, merge, and splinter.

That splintering has not been without ongoing internal debates peculiar to the vampiric state. One of the accusations that the non-psivamp sanguinarians leveled at the psychic vampires was that they tended to have stronger personalities and dominated the conversations, chasing some shyer types off of the email lists. This was entirely unsurprising, given the psivamp habit of attempting to run every interaction as if they were going to get lunch-energy out of it, even when it's impossible. (For the record, I do not believe that you can get prana from arguments on an email list, where even if you could somehow astrally tap into someone from across the country—and this is a whole lot harder and rarer than you'd think—the person who wrote that email did so hours ago, and is now waiting tables or taking tickets or sleeping. It's a classic case of catnip-response provoking behavior.)

The so-called online vampire community can be confusing to watch. The majority of individuals are not ethical psychic vampires; many or most may not be psychic vampires at all. There's a huge amount of deliberate—one might even say near-hysterical—identification with the twentieth-century mythical vampire archetype, because people find it romantic. (A psychologist friend of mine noted that part of the attraction of that Anne Rice-type archetype, especially for young people, is that the vampire never has to change in any way. In fact, s/he is rewarded for not growing or changing by becoming far more powerful, which of course is exactly the opposite of how things happen in real life.) Michelle recounts this problem in the hatchling vampire community:

> I don't know if you've noticed this trend or not, but I've watched a lot of people now grow up through the stages of accepting something different about themselves, and from vampires to Wiccans to gays, I've seen this early period, right after the guilty denial and the tentative acceptance, where the person just throws themselves headlong into that different identity. It's almost like they are trying to convince themselves that this is what they are, and in order to convince themselves, they go to all manner of extremes with it. Gays put rainbows and p-flags all over their homes, their clothes, their cars. They become vocal activists. They make a point of being 'out' in every aspect of their lives, sometimes to the point of bad taste. Wiccans and Pagans decorate their homes in Neo-Pagan chic. They put pentacles on their cars, pentacles on their cats' collars, pentacles dangling from their ears and every other available bit of body-jewelry, etc., ad nauseum.
>
> Vampires tend to go through a stage where they dress the part in order to "come out of the coffin" to everyone. They pale their faces and wear their sunglasses constantly. They hang ankhs around their necks, ankhs from their ears, they get ankh tattoos, bumper stickers, and so on. Some of them go so far as wearing capes and tooth-caps like they were casual wear, not just limiting such attire to clubs, but stomping out to Dennys at eleven o'clock at night in full regalia in spite of and perhaps because of the stares.
>
> Like a gay couple kissing in the middle of a Southern Baptist Church social, it's overkill. And on the surface it looks like it's meant for everyone around that person, but I think that stage is really for them. By inundating themselves so thoroughly

in that social identity, they are trying to accept it as a reality for themselves. So I think I proudly proclaimed myself a vampire when I was going through that rather awkward stage.

                                                            –Michelle

Some psychic vampires work with and love the "vampire aesthetic", seeing it as part of embracing the Darkness in a positive spiritual way. Others, like Sarah Dorrance, have problems with both the aesthetic and the community. Sarah comments that: "I find the vampire aesthetic of today amusing, since only a handful of people who indulge in it have an inkling of their cultural roots—the leftovers of the Romantic poets, of the Symbolist decadents, etc." She feels that the vampire lifestylers have laid down too hard a line, implying that theirs is the only "true" way to be a vampire of any kind, and thus turning off people who aren't comfortable with the archetype as interpreted by twentieth-century novelists and role-playing-gamers. She admits that online vampire communities can be a place for some psivamps—mostly younger ones—to find out about themselves, but says, "I have mixed feelings about this. Whenever something becomes popular, more people get access to discovering and expressing a part of themselves, but whenever a subculture is created, things often get rigid and conformist."

Doran, a self-professed psivamp and sanguinarian, says, "There's very little room in current vampire communities for people who want to look, very rationally, at what they are and how they got that way and what they can do about it, with all the vampire mythos stripped away. People really want there to be some kind of connection to the mythic vampire, beyond just the name and the ability to draw out life force. They want to think that doing this will make them glamourous and immortal and psychically powerful. Of course, this means that those of us who aren't even trying to fit that pattern don't have much space there, which is why I left."

It's true that there is a lot of power-tripping in some communities, with more charismatic and less ethical types creating "harems" of wide-eyed followers who are convinced that they can be "turned" into vampires, even over email. There are, however, some groups who seem to be honestly working with psychic vampirism as a legitimate form of energy moving for magical purposes. House Kheperu, for example, works with a triad-form circle of magical workers; "Counselors" draw energy out of the universal currents, "Priests" pull it out of them and shape it to the right intent, and "Warriors" create boundaries and ground the energy.

The modern vampire communities seem to revolve around the sanguinarians, which isn't inappropriate, as they were the ones who started those communities to begin with. Both those who do it for psivamp reasons and those who do it for other reasons point out that their political needs, as a community, are different from those of those who merely take prana. Calling yourself a psychic vampire in public will at worst result in people disbelieving you and perhaps thinking of you as a weirdo; some may even take it as a metaphor rather than a reality. Telling people that you consume human blood can get you labeled as a potentially violent lunatic; the coming-out danger is considerably worse, and getting publicly labeled as such can be a real hazard to your livelihood and safety. Seen in this light, it's not surprising that sanguinarians tend to feel that they have more in common with other sanguinarians than with strictly psychic vampires.

The word vampire itself is a difficult legacy. Some embrace it, with all its brutal, romantic, and mythical symbols, and others reject it entirely. Still, even those people who refuse to use the term often find themselves faced with it when they try to explain themselves: "You feed off of people's life force? You mean like a vampire?" It sometimes seems that there's no getting away from it, so we might as well say it up front.

Michelle points out that, "If I'm going to fulfill my mission of reaching out to others like myself and educating them so they can control their vampirism and choose to feed consciously from aware and willing donors, then I have to speak in the language that the majority of people will understand. These days, I see the V-word as a communication tool. It's not the best word for what I and others like me are, but it's the closest word we have in the English language. In more diverse communities, I try to use words that are still descriptive yet lack some of the shock-value that comes with the term vampire. Feeder and taker are two terms I've used with some success in describing what we are to New Age and other open-minded spiritual audiences."

Of course, usually one has to go through the rigors of explaining that even though we may use that word, we are not undead, we are not immortal, we do not grow fangs and turn into bats, we may actually like garlic, and holy water will not turn us away. Wiccans and Pagans have had similar issues in the past with regard to stereotypes of green-skinned, warted, pointy-hat-wearing, frog-enspelling creatures, so they may well understand our educational predicament.

One also has to take the brunt of suspicion for every unethical psivamp that ever sponged off the person you're coming out to. This is often the hardest thing. In most of the sort of circles where people will believe you when you say you're one, they will likely also assume that this means you're Evil. They are also unlikely to take your word for it when you say that you aren't. Others, reaching out with misplaced compassion, will want to "heal" you, and make your dependence on feeding go away. If you're a primary vampire, this is impossible to manage. If you're a secondary vampire, you can be considered at fault if you let it get away from you, but if you have it under control and aren't harming anyone, you might not consider it something that needs to be "fixed". Brushing away the well-meaning healers can get you fingered as "unenlightened".

Somehow, a change in attitude has to come around. Spiritual and psychic healing systems have to find a niche for psivamps where we can be useful and respected, and not necessarily always get stuck as the Dark Adversary, whether we like it or not. Playing the Dark Adversary can be fun, especially when it's being forced on you anyway, and you figure that you might as well say, "Boo!" and scare a few uptight people. It's tasty, too, if you thrive on that sort of energy, which can create a vicious cycle of scaring and feeding, positive reinforcement for bad behavior.

However, no matter how fun or filling it is, it also gets wearing after awhile. It's tiring to have people automatically distrust you. (Ask any underclass African-American who's had to shop in an expensive store. They'll tell you what a pain in the ass it is to be seen as the Adversary all the time.) It can cause isolation; although some psychic vampires may band together, many more are lonely social rejects. It also furthers harmful myths about our "cursed" status.

I'm not cursed. I fully believe that God/dess made me, everything that I am, for a purpose. I'm a tool, designed as specifically and deliberately as any healer. I am not a mistake, because S/he doesn't make them. It's time that we took this information to other communities. However, first we have to release our grip, just a little, on our obsessive love affair with being the Dark Adversary all the time. There have to be other ways to be what we are. For a thousand years, the archetype of "witch" meant someone who practiced evil magic and harmed people. The propaganda involved in creating that image is beside the point; it still made a strong impression on centuries of people. Much has been done by modern Neo-Pagans to reclaim that word and give it new meaning. It's our turn now, to do some reclaiming and rehabilitating of our image if we can. Are we up to that challenge?

12
The Astrological Vampire

(Note The following is geared to moderately experienced astrologers. If you are a newcomer to astrology, I suggest that you start with the book The Inner Sky *by Steven and Jodie Forrest, which explains things in as user-friendly a manner as possible. If you really need this explained to you right away, please bring this book to a professional astrologer.)*

As an astrologer, it has always been fascinating to me to look for the indicators of certain group characteristics in people's charts. No, I haven't found the definitive astrological hallmark of the vampire, but I've found a few things that seem to be common the charts of many vampires, both primary and secondary.

First, the planet Pluto does seem to have a bearing on the phenomenon of psychic vampirism. The energy that Pluto represents is complex and mysterious; its keyword is transformation, but its transformations are often painful. Pluto is about power; Pluto transits often herald power struggles. Pluto is about powerlessness; Pluto transformations sweep you away and force you to face parts of yourself that you had never touched before. Pluto is dark, but it forces hidden things up into the light.

Being a psychic vampire is a Plutonian experience. You have a power that you can use to take something from other people, but at the same time you struggle continually with its power over you. It is both a weapon and a tool, a need and a chain. It is intense, and so are we. Pluto is deeply linked with issues of power; its negative manifestation is tyranny, and its positive face is power over oneself and one's urges. We vampires are often control freaks to one extent or another, and we need to understand that if one does not have true control over oneself, all the attempts to control others with come to nothing. On the other hand, it is often true that the more inner power you develop, the less you find that you need to control others, and the more trust you have in the universe that your next meal will be sent to you.

This planetary force is named for the Greek god of death and the underworld, and we often find ourselves dealing with hidden, underground urges and feelings. Pluto has some things in common with the cultural myth of the vampire, and others that contradict it. On the one hand, the vampire myth does deal with death and pain and darkness, and it is heralded by a transformation. On the other hand, after that single transformation the mythic vampire continues basically unchanged, unlike Pluto's realm where transformations must continue periodically and eternally. No one gets to be steady-state in this turbulent world. Pluto is closer to the reality of the shamanic rebirth, where the individual is dismembered and comes back a different, wiser, and more connected person. Often this transformation comes with terrible trials and struggles. The struggle of a vampire to become aware and spiritually conscious—certainly a formidable struggle in and of itself—can be seen as a kind of shamanic Ordeal Path.

Quite a few vampires are born with a strongly-aspected Pluto. A secondary vampire may also learn to pull energy (which can feel like a kind of "awakening", if it's done consciously) during a Pluto transit. The strong currents of Pluto may shake someone awake to new skills, or deplete them into desperation until they cling to whatever prana they can get. Remember, however, that Plutonian energy is not there to destroy you, but to rebirth you into a new life. Look for the sign and house placement of your Pluto to get an idea where and how these rebirthings will happen.

Discipline, the subtext of this book, is ruled by Saturn, the unforgiving old man of the planetary spheres. Saturn is the force that says, "No." Well-disciplined vampires may have strong, positive Saturn aspects, such as trines. Other vampires without such aspects may end up forcibly coming to terms with their negative feeding behavior during a Saturn transit. No one can say that Saturn is exactly comfortable, but the "old man" of astrology can be the impetus that forces one to change one's life. Like Pluto, he is also associated with death, although he is closer to Thanatos than Hades—the Grim Reaper rather than the King of Death. It's not uncommon for Saturn to deliver someone into

Pluto's hands. Look for the sign and house placement of your Saturn to find the best methods for teaching yourself discipline.

The planet which seems to be the biggest enemy of ethical psychic vampires is Neptune. This is the planet, on one hand, of illusions, delusions, addictions, and insanity. On the other hand, it is also the planet of higher spirituality, of finding oneness with the Universe. Neptune is in charge of dissolving your boundaries and merging with something bigger than yourself, and that can be the Universal energy, or the bottle, or the aliens who gave you the tinfoil hat. I've found that vampires with strong Neptune aspects in their chart often have the hardest time with the Saturnian discipline necessary to create those good ethical boundaries. Neptune likes to flow, and it's all too easy for us to flow right into someone else, and we all know what comes after that. This doesn't mean that it's impossible for us, just difficult. Look to the sign and house position of Neptune for your danger zones.

Another astrological phenomenon which has barely been touched on in current research is the significance of black holes in an astrological chart. The only astrologer who seems to have been dealing with black holes is Philip Sedgwick, and even he isn't quite sure what to make of them. He theorizes that they have to do with such variable concepts as time travel, karmic flashbacks, and higher wisdom. However, I have found black holes prominently placed in the charts of the few vampires I've been able to get birth dates from, and I have to wonder if there's some connection there. This is especially telling as so many of us describe ourselves in black hole terminology when we're hungry.

From the Earth's point of view, black holes appear in clusters in specific limited areas. In reality, of course, they are millions of lightyears apart, but they "line up" from our perspective and look as if they clump together. This means that people who have planets at those degrees might have one, two or even three black holes near or on it. If those points are major planets such as the Sun or Moon, or even the ascendant, this can be a large dose of black-hole energy. It's possible, although untested, that black holes on any inner "personal" planet may cause primary psychic vampirism, or even a talent for secondary psychic vampirism. Inner planets, and especially the aforementioned three points, are the most likely culprits, however. It would be interesting to astrologically poll a number of vampires and see where the black holes were in relation to their major planets. I only have a few vampire charts to compare, including my own and my daughter's. I have three of the sixteen possible black holes in a cluster within a couple of degrees of my Sun, and one directly on my ascendant; my daughter has black holes conjunct her Jupiter, Mars, Mercury, and Uranus.

It's also possible that the conditions for secondary vampirism—either the traumatic experience or the consensual training—may occur during the progression of a major planet over a black hole. This may be an astrological "trigger" that allows the individuals' gift of moving energy to go in a new direction. Until more work is compiled on the astrological charts of different kinds of vampires, we can only theorize, but it's a compelling direction to move in.

Black Holes

Name	α	δ	β	λ 1950	λ 1980	λ 2000	Notes
Cygnus X-1	299 05 28	54 N 15	35 N 04	12 ≈ 56	13 ≈ 21	13 ≈ 38	Star HDE 226868, 3U1956 + 35, X-ray eclipsing, p * 5.6 days
CAS A	350 18 15	54 N 15	58 N 33	26 ♈ 42	27 ♈ 07	27 ♈ 24	3C 461, 3U2321 + 58, 300 yrs. old
Virga A	187 01 15	14 N 26	12 N 42	01 ♎ 05	01 ♎ 30	01 ♎ 47	ZS, M-87, NGC 4486, 3U1228 + 12
M-82	147 58 30	52 N 07	69 N 56	28 ♋ 17	28 ♋ 42	28 ♋ 59	NGC 3034
Vela XR-1	128 24 00	60 S 25	45 S 03	02 ♌ 43	03 ♌ 08	03 ♌ 25	Vela X, Pulsar 0833-45, 10^4—10^5 years old, 3U0838 - 45.
3U0900 - 40	135 03 45	53 S 56	40 S 22	06 ♍ 22	06 ♍ 47	07 ♍ 09	Star HD77581, X-ray eclipsing p = S.95 days, X-ray pulse = 284 sec.
Cen X-3	169 43 45	56 S 19	60 S 19	28 ♎ 31	28 ♎ 56	29 ♎ 13	3U1118 - 60, V799 Gentauri, X-ray eclipsing, p = 2.1 days X-ray pulse = 4.8 sec.
Cen A	200 36 00	31 S 20	42 S 45	06 ♏ 56	07 ♏ 21	07 ♏ 38	3U1322 - 42
Circinus X-1	229 11 00	37 S 15	56 S 59	03 ♐ 25	03 ♐ 50	04 ♐ 12	CIR X-1, 3U1516 - 56
Hercules X-1	253 18 00	57 N 33	35 N 36	04 ♐ 11	04 ♐ 36	04 ♐ 53	HZ Her, 3U1653 - 35, X-ray eclipsirg p = 1.7 days, X-ray pulse = 1.24 sec. X-ray 10-11 days on, 25 days off.
Sco X-1	244 16 45	05 N 43	15 S 32	05 ♐ 09	05 ♐ 34	05 ♐ 51	3U1617 - 15, V818 Scorpii
3U1700- 37	255 06 30	14 S 57	37 S 46	17 ♐ 52	18 ♐ 17	18 ♐ 34	Star HD153919, X-ray eclipsing p = 3.4 days
GX339-4	254 44 30	25 S 52	48 S 44	18 ♐ 53	19 ♐ 18	19 ♐ 35	3U1658 - 48
SGR X-4	275 06 30	07 S 01	30 S 23	04 ♑ 26	04 ♑ 51	05 ♑ 08	3U1820 - 30, Sgr 4, NGC 6624
SMC X-1	018 49 45	66 S 26	73 S 42	11 ≈ 39	12 ≈ 04	12 ≈ 31	SK160, 3U0115 - 73, X-ray eclipsing
Cygnus X-3	307 38 15	56 N 55	40 N 47	27 ≈ 53	28 ≈ 18	28 ≈ 35	3U2030 + 40, X-ray eclipsing p = 4.8 hours.

13
Related Energy-Moving Techniques

All over the world, there are energy-moving techniques that pull energy out of people for different reasons. There are shamanic techniques in tribal cultures, and more well-known methods such as Ch'i Gong, Reiki, or Huna. An example of an aboriginal practice of this type is the Inuit "weasel-pulling", where the shaman uses a weasel puppet to run over the patient's body and "eat" blockages and problems. These skills are not strange and arcane; they are part of an extensive "toolbox" of techniques used for moving energy around.

The people who use these tools don't call themselves vampires, as they don't necessarily do this stuff merely in order to feed themselves (although there are cautionary tales of "power-stealing" among tribal shamans). The main difference between a secondary vampire and an energy worker who draws out someone's negativity is how often they take for selfish reasons, even ethically. Some people can slip back and forth over the line over the course of their lives.

Anyone can learn these techniques, with a little work and care. It won't turn you into a vampire; that's a choice you will have to make yourself. There are good reasons for learning how to do it, and there are also good reasons not to do it. I'm including a brief outline for those who are interested, written with the excellent help of Tannin Schwartzstein, who has had ten years of doing energy work and eclectic healing.

One positive reason to use these techniques is for healing. Psychic energy drawing techniques, such as those vampires use, allow one to go much deeper into the aura than many other healing methods. This is precision work, and in the hands of an experienced practitioner it can be highly accurate at diagnosing problems on a close level. It can also increase sexual/emotional connections for long-term intimate relationships, although this aspect should be used with care; it's a lot harder to break up with someone with whom you have this kind of connection. You can use this skill to explore someone's energy body intimately, but remember that they might be able to learn a good deal about you as well.

Energy drawing work can also be used as a form of spiritual discipline. Learning sword-forms of the martial arts such as kendo, kenjitsu, or iaido can give you grace and focus, even if you don't ever intend to strike someone's head off. Similarly, learning these techniques can give your energy workings grace, balance, and versatility. It may not be the form of energy work that everyone wants to or even should use, but its addition to one's "toolbox" can add depth and knowledge to other methods. Giving energy to someone is idealized in the healing world, but sometimes it is necessary to take away as well. Energy drawing is yin to energy projection's yang, and you may need to do both in a single session. Even if you choose never to use these exercises as anything more than exercises, you should be aware that they do exist and are useful.

While there are no quick fixes in healing, sometimes you may need to pull something deep and nasty out of someone. There are things that all the smudging and flooding in the world will not reach, whereas an experienced drainer may be able to get in and suck it out. It can also work as a way to calm someone enough to actually do healing work on them. However, it is one of the more dangerous tools in the box, and requires extra care and practice. Keep in mind the witches' saying: What can kill, can cure.

Negative reasons, of course, are outlined in the rest of this book. It goes without saying that what goes for a primary vampire goes for a secondary vampire, or even someone who doesn't consider themselves any kind of a vampire but simply uses this skill on occasion for healing uses.

There are certain conditions that contraindicate energy draining— in other words, they will do you, the worker, more harm than any good you can do for others. One such category is people who suffer from chronic depression, as they will be exceptionally sensitive to negative "residue". If you aren't normally depressive but you're having a depressed episode, you should avoid pulling bad stuff out of people you're healing, as it might make it worse. (Two depressed people trading energy back and forth can make each other worse.) Another category is individuals who are often mentally unstable, or who are having an unstable episode in their life. Still another category is people who are frequently weak or sickly due to chronic illness, unless they have amazing willpower, as the urge to take more than is healthy may be overwhelming.

There's a difference between "drawing" and "draining" energy. It's like getting water from a well; when you draw up a bucket, that's all you're taking. When you're draining something, you're trying to get as much as you can. The former is a useful technique for helping others; the latter may be useful for helping yourself, but can be damaging if great care is not used.

This kind of energy working isn't the best thing to start with if you've never done any kind of energy work before. In order to work with it, you need to be reasonably familiar with basic energy moving, such as the classic "zen ball" and other simple techniques. While we do not have the time to go into these techniques here, you can refer to Chapter 2 of *The Urban Primitive*, or *Basic Psychic Hygiene* by Sophie Reicher for a basic primer in this kind of work.

For instance, you should know the anatomy of an energy body, which has outer layers (the aura and external energy meridians) and inner layers (the chakras and the internal energy meridians). If this concept is entirely new to you, you need to learn about basic energy anatomy from somewhere else—for instance, an entry-level Reiki or Ch'i-Gong course.

Before you start this technique, you should already be aware of your own energy—how it moves, whether it's hot or cold, etc. You will be extending your energy from some part of your body's aura; the fingers and hands are often the easiest places to "extend" because we are used to using them as tools. Other areas might be the inside of the wrist (a la Spiderman and his webs), the eyes, mouth, and sexual organs. (For what it's worth, many of the places that are the easiest to extend are also easy to get into as "ports".)

Your own knowledge of your energy flow will help the visualization of your extensions. Some popular and useful forms are creeping vines, tentacles, wires, or just extended body parts. Use what seems to come naturally to you. However, while these visualizations are useful to get started with, do not be distracted by them. They will place imaginative limits on the movement of your extensions that will eventually get in the way when it's time to move beyond them. For example, if you visualize your extensions are long hair flowing out from your head, it will eventually limit your energy reach to only around your head area.

Eventually you are going to want to move beyond the visualization and just do it automatically, without thinking. When you reach for a pen on the table, you don't think about how your arm is moving; you may not even be aware of your arm per se. You're focusing on the target, the pen, and that's what it should be like with your psychic extensions. Practice "tapping" on things, and concentrate not on what your tentacle/vine/wire is doing but on what it's feeling. Get a willing partner and "tap" all over their aura. See how far away you can get and still feel them. (Some people can sink a tentacle into someone's aura from across a room, but you'll find that the further away you are, the thinner the "tube" gets, so you're getting less from the same effort.)

Another reason for getting beyond visualization is that these techniques are about precision, not imagination. You really need to be able to feel the energy and know what that feels like to the point where there's no question something's actually happening. The nagging feeling of "am I just deluding myself" is only going to go away if you keep doing it and doing it until the sensations themselves are second nature. It's the way to tell if you are really doing something—that and working with a friend who can give you a running update of what it feels like on their end. You can use these techniques to reach into yourself and mess around, but it's difficult—Tannin describes it as "feeling like guitar feedback sounds".

When doing deep energy work of any kind, one needs to "find a way in". Do a scan of the body and check it out. When a healer does this, they are looking for "hot spots" that need healing. To draw energy, look for thin spots in the aura. If you're not an experienced scanner, you might look for areas of the body that have injuries, strains, or other physical problems. This is especially useful if you are actually looking for a way to give pain relief or some other sort of healing. (When looking for problem areas, you may be able to "feel" them as tactilely different, or you may be forced past them, like water flows around a stone in a stream.

After the working, you need to get the residue out of yourself. If the energy tastes especially bad and you don't want to risk absorbing any of it, you can dump the whole thing. If you've been using your hands and you feel like they are dirty, you can wave your hand an inch above a lit candle, and use the heat to caress your hand and burn the bad stuff off. Charging and keeping a special candle for this use is recommended. If you're not sure how to charge candles, see Chapter 2 of *The Urban Primitive*.

You can also use water as a post-working purification. Fill a bowl with water and add some light purifying oil such as lavender, citrus, or rose. You can place stones, crystals, or even just glass marbles in the bottom. Dip your hands into it, after or during the work, and let the energy run off. To dispose of it, dump it onto the earth, or down the toilet.

Ritual Permission

Create sacred space. You should have done your purifications first, before this exercise. If you like, you can come in together and do a final smudge over each other. Make some gesture of honoring each other, such as a bow or handshake or hug. Get into whatever position you intend to do the healing work in— lying down, sitting, etc.

The individual who is doing the work states their intent, e.g. "I intend to reach into your body and attempt to remove this blockage. Do you give me permission?"

The individual who is receiving the work should clearly state that they do. "Yes, you have my permission. Go ahead."

The worker thanks them, and goes ahead with the work. Afterwards, the worker checks in with the person that they are working on, and makes sure that they are all right. Aftercare for a healing where energy drawing is used is just as important as—and much the same as—aftercare for a feeding.

One interesting exercise to do with a willing partner is to sink an extension into their aura (with their permission) and slip it into their blood vessels, following the flow of the circulatory system. See if you can "travel" up and down their system. If you can pick out the system of energy meridians, you can use that, but for most people who aren't familiar with the energy meridian system, the circulatory system is a good place to begin. (There are places where the blood vessels run with the meridian system; for example, the "port" in the inside of the wrist is right on the place where you'd probably slice if you wanted to kill yourself. Sometimes they are completely separate, however—the "port" in the neck is not right on either the jugular or the carotid; it's farther back, on the edge of the trapezius muscle.)

When you travel inside someone's energy system, you not only pick up stuff, but you also leave stuff behind, so you can "infect" someone if you're not careful. For instance, if you're sick or angry or dislike the person, that can rub off. While it's nice to think that you can filter out anything nasty, the truth is that the average secondary vampire is moving too fast to divert concentration into such things. Think of yourself as a hypodermic needle being inserted into someone. You wouldn't do that without taking sterile precautions, and likewise you should take the same precautions for energy work. Although these techniques mimic the work of a primary psychic vampire, they do not guarantee you the kind of energy-transformation that protects primary vampires from psychic indigestion, so regular cleansing is imperative.

Since the first thing you can control is yourself, so you will want to do some preparations. Before you even walk into the room and do this, sit quietly and assess your mood. Nobody's perfect, and nobody expects you to be the Buddha while doing this, but when you have time to plan it's better to do it. Do whatever grounding and centering you need to feel at least somewhat serene; if you are the type who prefers to do your energy work on an empty stomach, do extra grounding to keep from being spacey. The less cleaning you do beforehand, the more you will need to do afterwards.

For those of you who do Reiki or some related technique, "comb" or "scrape" your aura to remove as much gunky energy as possible. If you like, you can light a candle, hold your hand close to (but not in) the flame after each "scrape" in order to burn it off. You can also use ice water to wash the energy. Repeat this until the entire body is wiped off. Some traditions feel that being naked makes the purification more effective, but we don't find it necessary. Smudging can help, but you have to actually do the energy work while you're waving the smoke around. If fasting works well for you, try it, as long as it doesn't make you too lightheaded. *(Raven's note: If you're hypoglycemic or diabetic, don't fast. Try a few days of a raw-food diet—raw fruit, vegetables, raw fish, milk and yogurt, especially unpasteurized fresh farm milk and yogurt, nothing processed. I'm hypoglycemic and I find that this works well as a substitute "light" fast for people who can't fast for medical reasons.)*

Your donor/client may want to do some purification as well; an herbal bath or smudge might be a good idea. However, be careful that you don't use "protective" herbs and oils such as: frankincense, myrrh, dragon's blood, amber, or cedar, as that will strengthen the shields, and you don't want to make your job harder. Concentrate on essences that calm and soothe but are not shield-building. Fasting may make some people's shields thinner, and others thicker; you may have to experiment in order to find the best combination of purification for your donor. Basically, the same methods used for cleaning the feeder will work for the donor. The point of all this is to get each of you as "clean" as possible so that neither party exchanges too much residue.

Once you've actually found your way into someone's energy system, you can immediately start drawing. Your connection is like a an electrical wire or a very thin tube through which energy can pass. The energy is going to be moving around your connection anyway, since energy is not static. Now start taking long, slow, deep breaths. On the in-breath, try to draw in their energy. On the out-breath, rest and do nothing. You are not trying to send anything out just yet. The prana may feel like different sensations to different people; to some it tingles, to others it burns or is like heat. Still others may feel nothing at all.

As it goes into your body, it will mix with your own energy and you will absorb it. If it feels uncomfortable, stop. *When in doubt, back out.* On the out-breath, visualize stopping up your tubes, and start pulling your connection back out. If it feels sticky, don't panic; the other person is unlikely to be able to keep your connection in them, as the natural reflex of their aura is to push you out. Just keep doing it again and again, slowly backing out little by little until it is entirely back in your body. If it feels good, take only a small amount and don't get greedy. Then pull out using the above method. Checking in with your patient throughout the treatment is a good idea, and any patient who seems unable to respond for any reason is a problem. Pull out and find out what's wrong.

If you don't get everything out and some of your connection gets stuck there, it's not a disaster. A purification on the part of the donor can flush it out, or they may absorb it. If this happens frequently, you can end up with a psychic connection to the person, which you may or may not want. (There are Tantric techniques where both people simultaneously draw out each others' energy and put it back, and we've wondered whether some of the mistaken "soulmate" experience is actually residue left over from unconscious forms of this dual energy working.) If you get too tangled up with someone, you may need to do a ritual severing.

Ritual Severing

This is for when you've developed a connection with someone due to energy exchange, and you want to get rid of a bond for whatever reason. Sometimes we bond to people who are not necessarily good for us. For example, if you got involved with a recovering addict who has slipped back into their addiction, and their addictive urges are traveling back along the connection to you, and you find yourself uncharacteristically wanting to do their drug (a situation that we've seen happen more than once) you'll want to let go of them in order to be healthy.

First, create sacred space, however that works for you. You will need the following: Some sort of symbolic or actual blade (your athame will do if you don't mind using it for this sort of thing). Make sure it's not unwieldy, because you will not be cutting flesh, even accidentally. Some kind of purification incense, such as dragon's blood or copal or vetiver—something heavy and somber. (Fresh organic tobacco can be used if no one in the room is allergic or quitting smoking.)

You and the person you are severing from should enter the space together. Acknowledge each other with a bow or a handshake, or some other courteous gesture. Stand or sit, facing each other. If necessary, you can have a third party do the severing; this works well if the "umbilical cord" between the two people is pictured as being in an awkward area.

Each person should bluntly state that they are no longer willing to be connected by this psychic bond, and that they feel that it must go. It is very important that both parties, if present, say this separately and in their own words. Now each person should concentrate on the connection itself, feeling it strongly and charging it with active energy like a live wire between them. The third party (or both people holding the blade together) should make a cutting gesture between both bodies, severing the cord. The remaining cord should then be pulled in to each person and sealed up; one way to ritually do this is to light a candle and wave it a couple of inches away from the skin, "cauterizing" the wound.

Then both people state that they are now separate, and no longer one on the psychic level. Close the sacred space, go to separate spaces where you cannot see, hear, or sense each other, and ground and center. Once you've ritually severed, stay away for a while. This ritual does leave a wound, and in order to heal properly, you need to get distance. When the scars are fully healed, you'll be able to face them again without restimulating the connection.

The healing from this ritual can take days, or weeks, or months. A feeling of loss and grief is common and doesn't mean that it didn't work. Grieving for twenty minutes or twenty days is fine and appropriate; you may need to acknowledge pain. However, within a very short time one should feel as if one's energy is one's own, and that one's aura is whole and single again.

In order to do this ritual when only one person is available, one has to be a bit harsher. Start the ritual as above, and then visualize the other person as clearly as you can in your mind. Using a photo is acceptable. State your intent clearly, out loud, to the universe. Do not justify anything, just say what you are doing. For example, "I don't want to be one with you any more," or I no longer want to be a part of your life, your body, or your soul," or "I have my own issues to deal with. Yours are no longer welcome in my body." Do not do this ritual for the purpose of revenge; this is more like a funeral than like counting coup. Visualize the cord and cut it as above.

Now imagine putting up a wall, or perhaps a thick second skin, in the direction of the other person. It is all right to be a little psychically insensitive for a time while you let this wound heal.

The biggest decision in using energy drawing techniques is not how to do it but when. As noted before, this can help with deep psychic problems that are apparent in the internal aura but are not affected by gentler means such as purifications or energy flooding. Always use your diagnostic tool first, and don't be too eager to go ripping it out unless you're sure that it isn't welded to something vital. You can do this for a general cleaning as well, where there is nothing specific wrong except general gunk to be removed. This technique is surgical cleaning, used to bust blockages and clean out specific centers; a scalpel rather than a scrub brush.

This is never something that you can do and get away scot-free. Not only must your patient trust you, but you have to trust your patient as well. Sometimes, when you're embedded in someone, if they also know these techniques (or are some flavor of vampire), they can start draining you instead. Then it becomes a power struggle—to pull out, or to win—which is neither useful nor healing.

Sometimes you may be asked to do energy removal on someone, and you don't feel comfortable about it. If they are referred by another person, ask them if they've worked with them and if they're all right. Some people are just addicted to the energy drawing; some people think that it will suck out all their problems and they use it as an excuse not to work on their issues. Don't feel obligated to work on anyone who you dislike, or who gives you the creeps.

If, while you're inside someone, you hit something that feels like a cold empty void that gives you vertigo and makes your stomach drop, pull back. This phenomenon can be attributed to a variety of things, including a kind of defense for a very emotionally sensitive area, or it can be a hungry place that needs energy and might attempt to suck yours. Another sort of place to avoid is something that feels like a hole that becomes a long tunnel extending out of that person and into another dimension. This is often found physically at the back of their head. Don't try to follow it, because you don't know what's on the other end. This "wormhole between worlds" is often found in people who had strong connections to some deity/daemon/spirit/what-have-you that visited their body rather often, and had built a "door". It can be the mark of someone who is a "horse" for one of the faiths that involve god-possession, or someone who is frequently in communion with some sort of guardian spirit, or someone who is possessed by something else, which we do not have the room to speculate on. Either way, to attempt to go through that door can get you possessed as well.

Again, I will stress that although these techniques can be used for vampirism, that's entirely your choice. Be careful, take things slowly, and try to do as little harm as possible.

Epilogue: In Conclusion

Child of mine,
Hunger is real
But it is a challenge,
Not an excuse.

Thirst is real,
But it is a trial,
Not a justification.

Need is real,
But it is a reason,
Not an absolution.

Nourishment is real,
But it must be paid for,
Not stolen.

The enemy is real,
But it lies within you
Not without.

Your power is real,
But it is a tool,
Not a weapon,
Given to you for a use,
Not an abuse.

Child of mine, I would hold you
and feed you forever
but I am not the God/dess
and S/he will not tell me
where your steps may lead.

May you find a way
May your wits be up to the game
May your imagination aid you
May your strength hold you back
And your judgment stay your hand
Until the right moment.
May every body of whirling sparks,
Every flowing fountain of energy,
Never cease to wear a human face,
Speak with a human voice,
And show you human needs.

Child of mine,
May you remember that power
Is greatest
When it need not be used.

Resources

Books That Might Actually Be Useful to Psychic Vampires

Belanger, Michelle. *The Psychic Vampire Codex.* Weiser Press, 2004.

The psychic energy work handbook of House Kheperu. Written for "Kheprian" vampires, but may be of use to others as well. Has some good basic energy-work exercises.

Belanger, Michelle (editor). *Vampires In Their Own Words.* Llewellyn Publication 2007.

Anthology of various kinds of vampires, writing about their own personal beliefs and the evolution of vampire communities.

Reicher, Sophie. *Basic Psychic Hygiene.* Ellhorn Press, 2008.

For those who want to learn how to shield themselves, or to clean out psychic gunk, this is a good primer.

Online Useful Vampire Sites

I'm hesitant to include online resources and websites, largely because the Internet is such a radically shifting place that by the time a book full of Internet sites has been published, it's not uncommon for half of them to have moved or been taken down. Still, I shall bravely list a few basic sites, in the hopes that they will be long-lived enough to be useful. In this I am grateful for the aid of Lono Vespertilio, who runs the first website listed below and whose reviews of various sites inform many of the reviews below.

The Psychic Vampire Resource and Support Page
http://psychicvampire.org/index.htm

While it's a bit rough around the edges, this site has a polyglot of information for new psychic vampires, from definitions for common terms to lessons in grounding, centering, and shielding, to healthful ingredients for Smoothies for picky-appetite vampires! Lono is easy to reach and willing to help people. The site is still growing, a work in progress.

Sanguinarius: For Real Vampires
http://www.sanguinarius.com

The first and best resource for sanguinarian vampires, run by Sanguinarius, an old hand on the scene. Psychic vampires who do blood-drinking may want to check it out.

The Vampire/Donor Alliance
http://www.darksites.com/souls/vampires/vampdonor/main.html

This site is older and rarely updated these days; it's the home site of Sarah Dorrance, who has her fingers in many pies. The Vampire/Donor Alliance is a loose-knit group of vampires and the people who feed them, with occasional national events.

House Kheperu
http://www.kheperu.org

House Kheperu is one of the best-known vampire houses and one of the older websites, having been in existence since 2001. The site contains wonderful information on the Kheprian path. Founder Michelle Belanger is author of *The Psychic Vampire Codex*, *The Psychic Energy Codex* and many more books on the subject of vampirism. Unfortunately, due to the burnout effect that forums have, it seems that kheperu.org has decided to close their forums permanently.

–Lono Vespertilio

The Path of the Kherete
http://www.kherete.org/houses.php

A relatively new website filled with information/ articles and a forum. The website is dedicated to those that follow the teachings of House Kheperu. The Kherete path is not specifically for psychic vampires, and allows sanguines and Otherkin to join in discussion and form houses. Kherete.org tends to be relatively strict with grammar; so you'll want to dust off your English 101 book before posting.

–Lono Vespertilio

SphynxCat's Real Vampires Support Page
http://sphynxcatvp.nocturna.org/index.html

One of the most useful sites I have found is this site by Sphynxcat. The site has been up and running since 1999, making it one of the oldest sites on psychic vampirism. Within the site you will find a plethora of well written and crafted articles for psychic vampires. I consider this site the number one source for information on vampiric health. The site is often updated and kept current. One of the downsides of this site is that there is no forum to trade information and converse with the community. However, the owner offsets this by making herself readily accessible through her IRC channel.

−Lono Vespertilio

By Light Unseen

http://bylightunseen.net/

One of the oldest sites and still one of the most current and up to date sites, with valuable information, articles, and reviews on other sites. While this site doesn't focus on community building, it puts its focus directly on solid information; whether you like it or not.

−Lono Vespertilio

The Voices of the Vampire Community

http://www.veritasvosliberabit.com/

This site is a valuable resource containing information from a wide cross section of the vampire community. One of the most valuable aspects of this site is the media section which contains all sorts of links to vampires in the media, articles, interviews, and television appearances.

−Lono Vespertilio

Ordo Sehkemu

http://www.ordo-sekhemu.org/

Ordo Sehkemu is one of the few sister houses of House Kheperu; though the focus of the website is on the Sekhrian and Luciferian path. The site contains excellent content and well written articles. The site does have a Yahoo group forum, in order to ask questions.

−Lono Vespertilio

About The Author

Raven Kaldera is a Northern Tradition shaman, homesteader, diviner, astrologer, herbalist, FTM intersexual activist, founder of the Neo-Pagan First Kingdom Church of Asphodel, and the author of far too many books and articles to list here. He can be found on a variety of websites, including ravenkaldera.org, northernshamanism.org, and cauldronfarm.com. 'Tis an ill wind that blows no minds.

CPSIA information can be obtained at www.ICGtesting.com
Printed in the USA
BVOW041753070212

282408BV00001B/30/P

9 780578 007908